FACTS AND FIGURES

A Practical Approach to Statistics

David Baker

The Anthony Gell School, Wirksworth, Derbyshire

Stanley Thornes (Publishers) Ltd

Text © David Baker 1989

Original line illustrations © Stanley Thornes (Publishers) Ltd 1989

All rights reserved. No part of this publication may be reproduced or transmitted in any form or by any means, electronic or mechanical, including photocopy, recording, or any information storage and retrieval system, without permission in writing from the publisher or under licence from the Copyright Licensing Agency Limited. Further details of such licences (for reprographic reproduction) may be obtained from the Copyright Licensing Agency Limited, of 33-4 Alfred Place, London WC1E 7DP.

First published in 1989 by:
Stanley Thornes (Publishers) Ltd
Old Station Drive
Leckhampton
CHELTENHAM GL53 0DN
England

British Library Cataloguing in Publication Data

Baker, David
   Facts and figures: a practical approach to statistics
   1. Statistical mathematics
   I. Title
   519.5

ISBN 0-7487-0040-4

Typeset by Tech-Set, Gateshead, Tyne & Wear.
Printed and bound in Great Britain at The Bath Press, Avon.

CONTENTS

	Preface	iv
1	**SO WHAT ARE STATISTICS?**	1
	What are statistics? — Who collects statistics and why? — So now what do we do with them? — So that's what we do with them! — Reading diagrams	
2	**DRAWING YOUR OWN DIAGRAMS**	19
	Bar charts — Pictograms — Pie charts — Stem and leaf plots — To sum up	
3	**AVERAGES AND RANGES**	37
	Averages — What's your average? — Showing the mean on a diagram — The median — The mode — Does the average tell it all? — Ranges — Some experiments to try	
4	**THE TRUTH, THE WHOLE TRUTH, AND NOTHING BUT THE TRUTH?**	53
	Advertising — Averages and percentages	
5	**PERCENTAGES AND SCATTERGRAMS**	66
	Percentages — Percentage strips — Percentage pie charts — Scattergrams	
6	**FURTHER STATISTICAL METHODS**	81
	Cumulative frequency curves — Histograms — Averages from grouped data	
7	**STATISTICAL PROJECTS**	99
	Thinking of a question — Deciding what data to collect — Questionnaires — Sampling — Bias — Collecting the data — Presenting your results — Analysing results and presenting conclusions — Ideas for projects	
8	**QUESTIONS FOR EXTRA PRACTICE AND REVISION**	109
	Index	124

PREFACE

The first four chapters of this book are designed to provide a simple and practical introduction to statistics for lower secondary or middle school children. It is hoped that the approach will prove both interesting and informative and will encourage children to look at statistics in a critical and informed way. It can be used alongside a general maths course, either to supplement its content or to provide a newer, more practical and more enjoyable approach to this important area of the mathematics curriculum.

The second four chapters include all the techniques required for GCSE mathematics, although not all of the methods are required by all of the boards. It is hoped that Chapter 7 will provide ideas for both teachers and students for coursework either for exam or school use. The final chapter contains extra questions of the type found in the first six chapters. These can be used either for revision or for extra practice throughout the book.

My thanks go to Jason and Stephen for their help with the original diagrams, to my colleagues at Anthony Gell for their encouragement and to the staff of Stanley Thornes.

David Baker
1989

1 SO WHAT ARE STATISTICS?

WHAT ARE STATISTICS?

Statistics are simply facts that involve numbers. They come in many different forms. Lots of people collect and use statistics for all kinds of different reasons.

To look at an everyday example, think of your school. Statistics are collected each day to find out how many people are at school.

Question 1

How is this done?

Question 2

Try to think of two reasons *why* these statistics are collected.

Question 3

Can you think of different ways in which these numbers could be collected each day?

Discussion 1

Try to think of other statistics which are collected by your school.
Discuss *how* and *why* each set is collected.

WHO COLLECTS STATISTICS AND WHY?

Let's look at some other people who need statistics.

Television companies (BBC and ITV) collect statistics each day to find out how many people they think are watching their programmes. Obviously they can't talk to everybody in the country every day, so they ask a small number of people to get an idea and then scale up the results. This is an example of a survey.

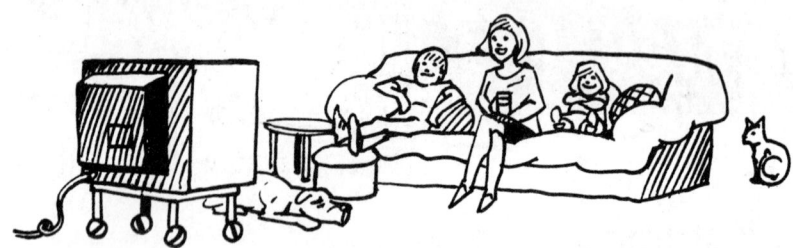

Discussion 2

The organisation which collects the statistics for the BBC and ITV is called BARB. How do they make sure that they don't just interview people who watch BBC 2?

How do they scale up the figures?

Try to find out what the letters BARB stand for and what the current 'top' programmes are on each channel.

A market research company called Gallup collects statistics on how many records are sold each week.

Question 4

How do they do this? Do they count *every* record sold in the country?

Question 5

What are these statistics used for?

Question 6

How do you usually see (or hear) them?

Large chains of shops also collect statistics. They want to know how much each shop in each town has sold that day or that week and whether more stock is needed. They may also want information about the staff.

> **Discussion 3**
>
> Try to think of what information the people in head office might want to know about the staff.
>
> What do you think they would need all the sales figures for?

All the big political parties collect statistics, for example, by asking people who they are likely to vote for. Local councils collect statistics about shopping and road facilities and doctors may like to know the number of people in an area who smoke. Scientists also collect statistics. They often have to make very accurate measurements and then sort out and display their results.

Question 7

Think of three more people or organisations who collect statistics. For each one, try to say *why* they need these figures and *how* they would get them.

SO NOW WHAT DO WE DO WITH THEM?

Once all the questions have been asked, figures added up or lengths measured, what do we do with all the numbers?

Let's look at a simple example of a survey:

We asked 50 school pupils to write down their current favourite children's television programme. They wrote their answers on a sheet of paper, a copy of which is shown on the next page — it looks a bit messy!

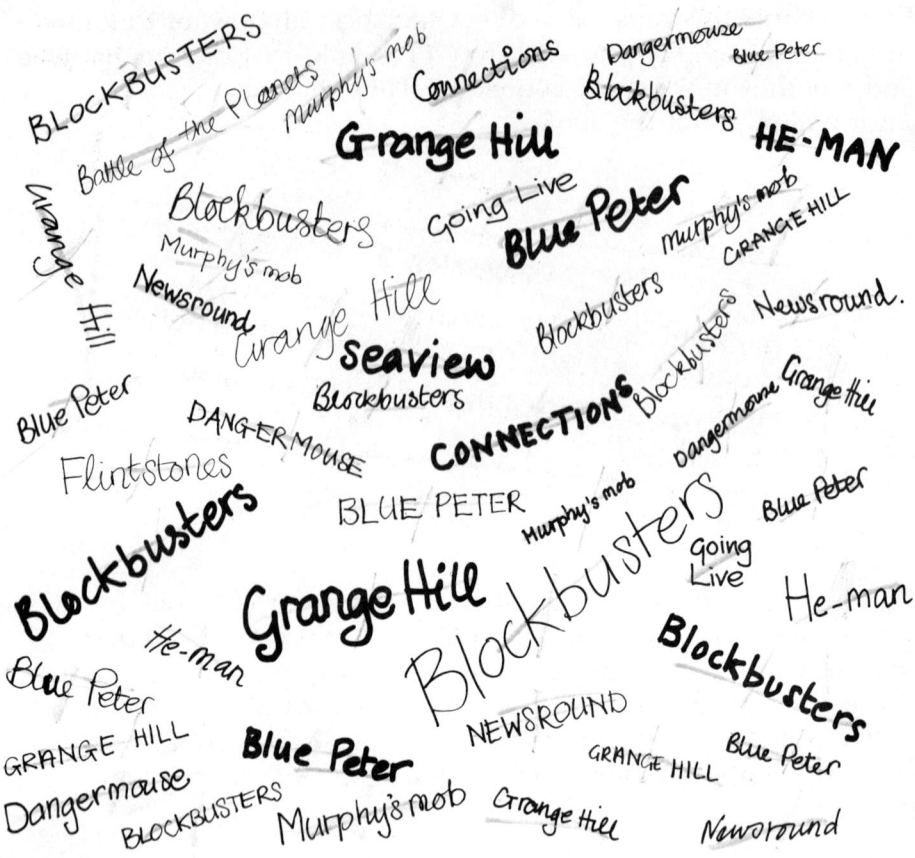

Figure 1.1

Question 8

Can you tell easily from this which are the top ten programmes?

Your answer to that question was probably no. All the information is too jumbled up to be easy to read. It needs sorting out!

To sort out information like this we often use a **tally chart**. This puts together all the people who gave the same answer, so that it is much easier to total them up.

It is not usually a good idea to go through all the data, looking for all the people who said, for example, *Grange Hill*, because this means that you then have to go through the list over and over again as you look for each different programme.

It is much better to go through the list just once, making a note of all the programmes you came across and making a mark by each one every time you come across it.

Discussion 4
What does the word *data* mean?

We have started a tally chart for our survey. Notice that there is a mark like this | each time we find a programme, so ||| means that so far we have found 3 people who like *Blockbusters*.

Programme	Tally	Total
Blockbusters	|||	
Grange Hill	||	
Blue Peter	|||	

Question 9

How many people do you think 卌 stands for?

Question 10

Why do you think the tally marks are grouped like this?

Question 11

What number does each of the following stand for?

(a) 卌 卌 卌 |||
(b) 卌 卌 卌 卌 卌 ||
(c) 卌 卌 卌 卌 卌 卌 卌 ||||

ACTIVITY 1

Complete the tally chart for our television survey. To begin with you will not know how many different programmes there are altogether so make sure you leave plenty of room to add programmes to your list as you find them. When you have gone through all the data, put the total for each programme in the Total column.

Question 12

What methods could you use to check that you have included all the children's answers? Use one method to check your results.

You should now have a completed tally chart which looks something like the one below. (Your titles may not be in the same order as ours.)

Programme	Tally	Total
Blockbusters	IIII IIII	10
Grange Hill	IIII IIII	9
Blue Peter	IIII III	8
Connections	II	2
He-man	III	3
Flintstones	I	1
Battle of the Planets	I	1
Newsround	IIII	4
Dangermouse	IIII	4
Seaview	I	1
Murphy's Mob	IIII	5
Going Live	II	2

Discussion 5

What advantages does the tally chart have compared with the original data?

Imagine that we had asked 500 people for their views, rather than 50.

Question 13

In what ways do you think the list might change? What problems would these changes cause for someone trying, for example, to put the programmes in order of popularity?

It is usually much more difficult to get information from a tally chart if it has a lot of information in it. For example, here is a chart of just 20 different pop singers and groups.

Frequency chart to show results of pop survey

Artist	Frequency	Artist	Frequency
George Michael	65	Pet Shop Boys	61
Kate Bush	31	David Bowie	30
Madonna	80	Genesis/Phil Collins	58
Eurythmics	32	Sting	45
Dire Straits	57	Nik Kershaw	50
U2	76	Samantha Fox	41
Status Quo	43	Michael Jackson	35
Duran Duran	54	Boy George	48
Five Star	69	Spandau Ballet	38
Bruce Springsteen	46	Depeche Mode	37

Note that we have used the word **frequency** instead of **total**. This word is often used in statistics to mean how many there are of something or how often something occurs. **Freq.** is sometimes used as a shortened version.

ACTIVITY 2

Try to work out which is the fifth most popular in the list. Now try to find the tenth most popular and get a friend to time how long it takes you.

As you can see, it takes some time to look through the list — and there are only 20 items in this list. The more items you have, the longer it takes. What would it be like if there were 100 entries?

To get around this problem, these simple tally charts are often used to make up different sorts of diagrams. Finding answers to questions then becomes much easier. There are lots of different types of chart and some of them are shown in the diagrams on the next few pages. You will see how to draw these charts in the next chapter.

Look at each one carefully, then try to answer the questions.

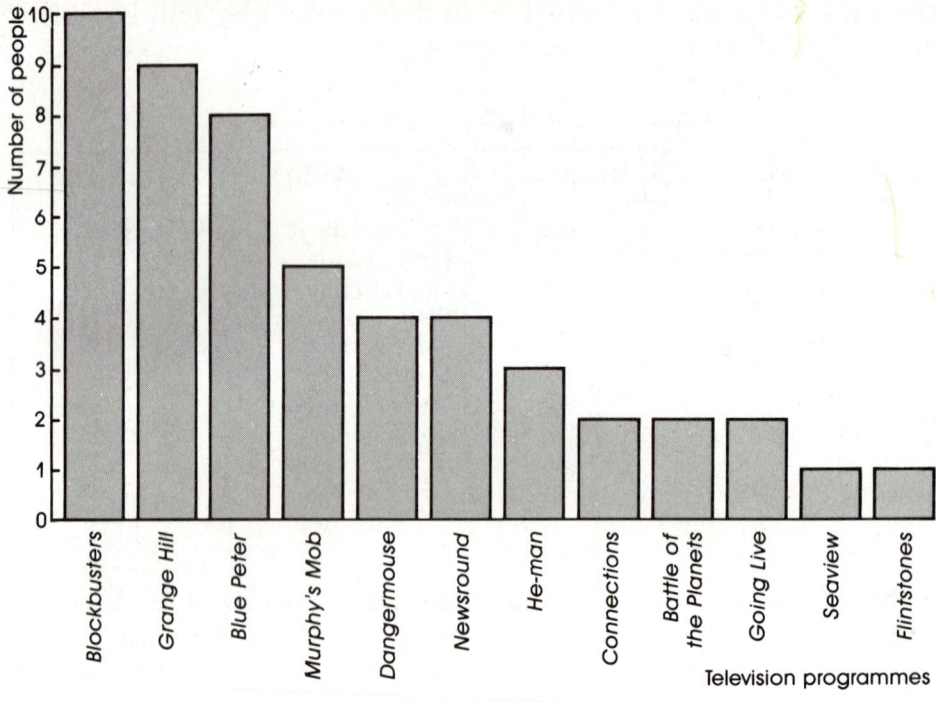

Figure 1.2

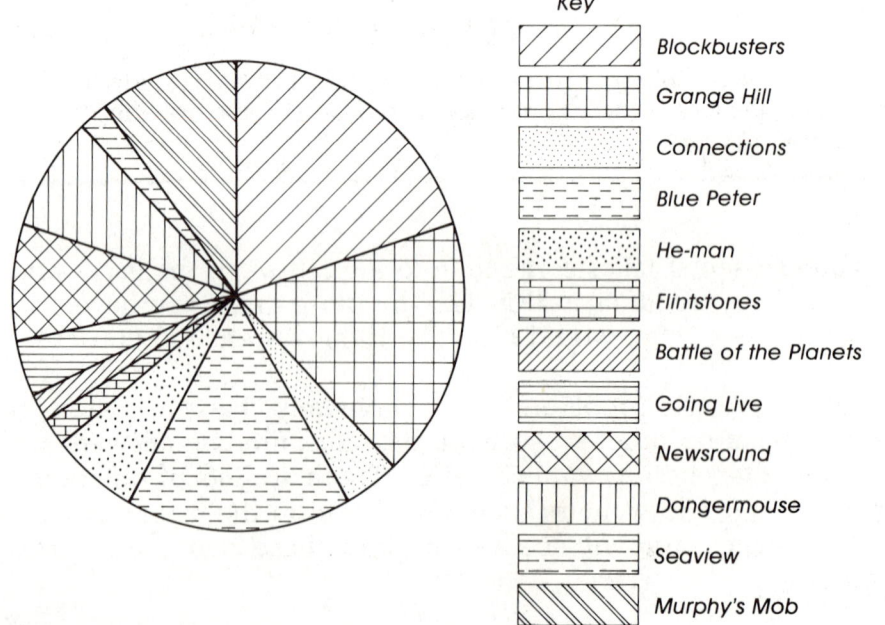

Figure 1.3

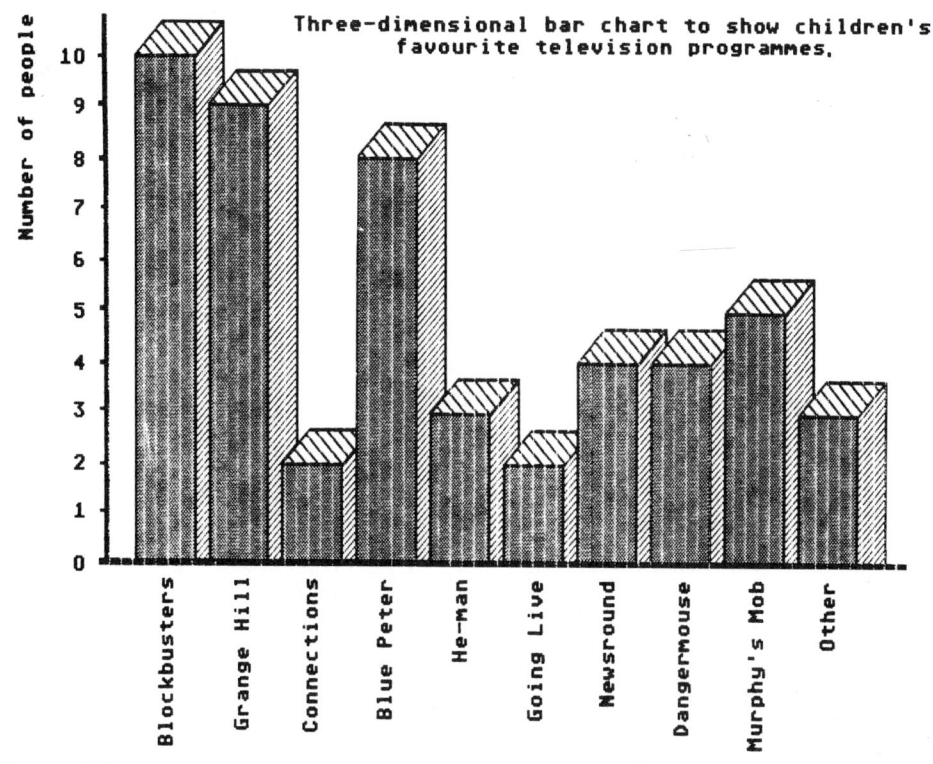

Figure 1.4

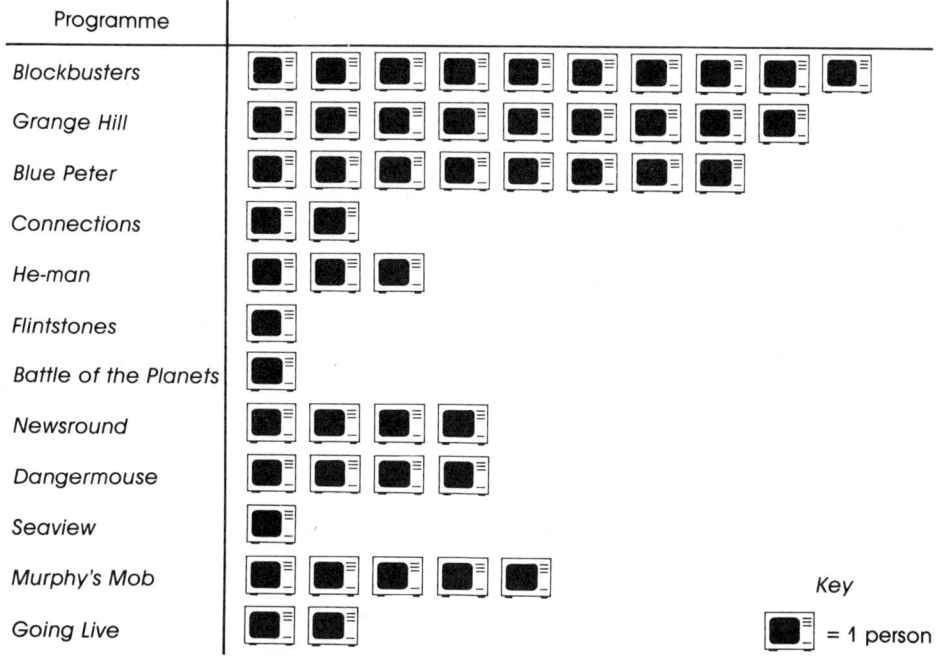

Figure 1.5

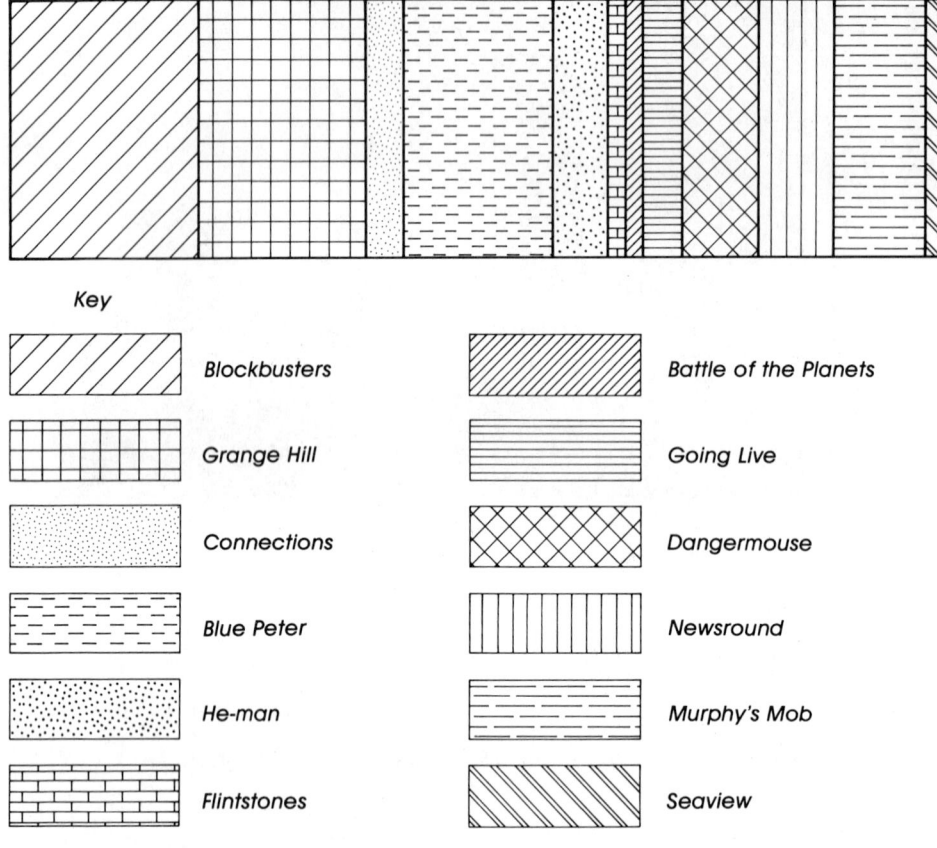

Figure 1.6

These questions ask you for your *views* about the diagrams. There are not really any right or wrong answers. When you have decided what you think, discuss your answers with the rest of the class.

Question 14

Which of the diagrams do you like the most and why?

Question 15

Which diagram shows the most popular programme the most clearly?

Question 16

Which diagram would make it the easiest to write down the top ten programmes and why?

Question 17

Which diagram is best for reading accurate figures of how many people liked each programme?

Question 18

Which diagram is best if you must want a quick overall view of the order?

ACTIVITY 3

For each of the diagrams, try to write down one advantage and one disadvantage. You can write down more if you wish. Discuss your answers.

We have seen that diagrams and charts can make groups of numbers much easier to read and understand. A good diagram should help anyone to see, almost at a glance, what is going on.

Remember, when you come to collect your own statistics and draw your diagrams, that the person who is looking at them should be able to tell quickly and easily what information the diagrams are trying to get across.

SO THAT'S WHAT WE DO WITH THEM!

We have now seen the process of collecting and presenting statistics. It can be summarised in the following easy stages:

Stage 1:
Decide what the problem or question is.

Stage 2:
Decide what statistics need collecting.

Stage 3:
Decide how to collect the statistics and try out your method to see if it works. If not, try another.

Stage 4:
Collect the statistics.

Stage 5:
Organise your answers and group them together. Often a table of some kind or a tally chart is useful here.

Stage 6:
Choose the best sorts of diagrams to show your results and produce them as neatly and attractively as possible.

Let's just check that these stages work:

ACTIVITY 4

We have done stage 1 from our list; that is we have thought of a problem:

A person who is very interested in insects decides that she would like to discover how many of each kind of butterfly live in the north of England. Clearly she can't count them all (they wouldn't all stay still!) so she will have to find some other way. Go through the other stages listed above to solve this problem.

See if you can think through the rest of the stages and then discuss your answers with the rest of your class or group.

If you wish, you could decide on another problem for yourself and try to fit our stages to it.

READING DIAGRAMS

Once some diagrams have been drawn, you need to be able to read them. On the next few pages you will find diagrams which we have drawn. There are some questions about each one. Look at the diagrams carefully before you answer the questions.

First of all, look at the bar chart of the rainfall for the first six months of 1988 (Figure 1.7).

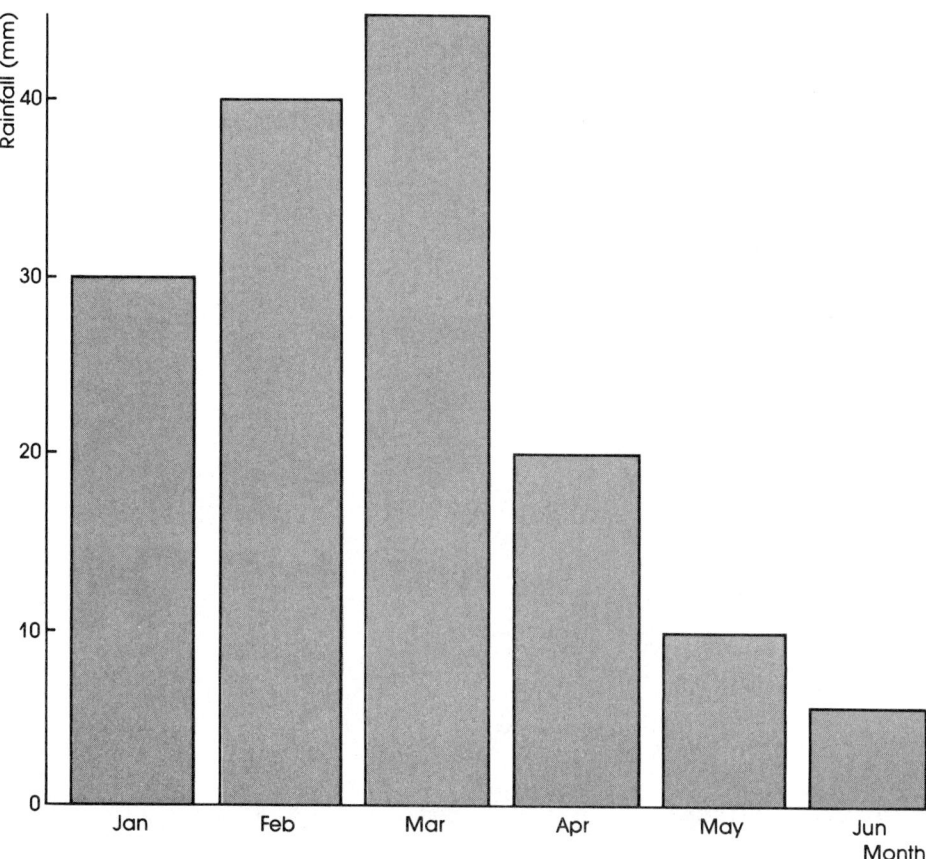

Figure 1.7

Question 19

In which month was there the most rain? In which was there the least?

Question 20

In which *two* months added together was there about the same amount of rainfall as in February?

Question 21

List the months in order according to amount of rainfall, starting with the month with the greatest.

Now look at the graph which shows the sales of Whisko soap powder during 1988 (Figure 1.8).

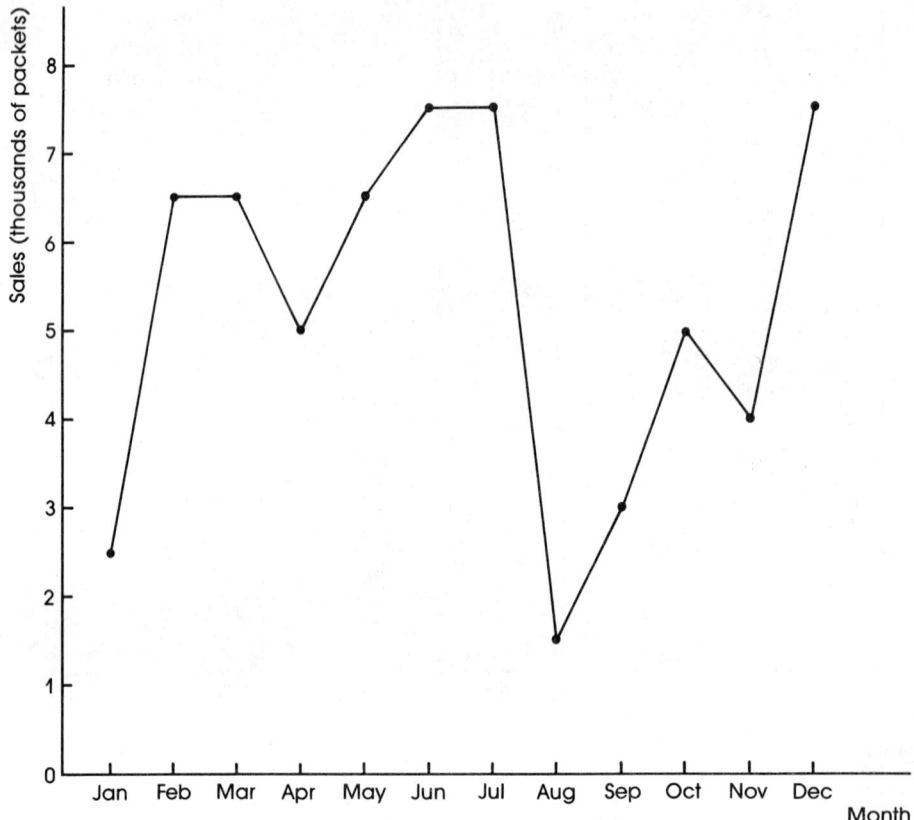

Figure 1.8

Question 22

In which month was the least amount of Whisko sold?

Question 23

How much was sold in this month?

Question 24

In which *three* months was the most Whisko sold?

Question 25

From March to April, the sales of Whisko fell. Name *two* other times during the year when this happened.

Question 26

How many packets of Whisko were sold in the first six months of the year? Was this more or less than the amount sold in the second six months, and by how much?

Next, look at the pie chart showing the spending of Dexborough County Council in the year 1987/88 (Figure 1.9).

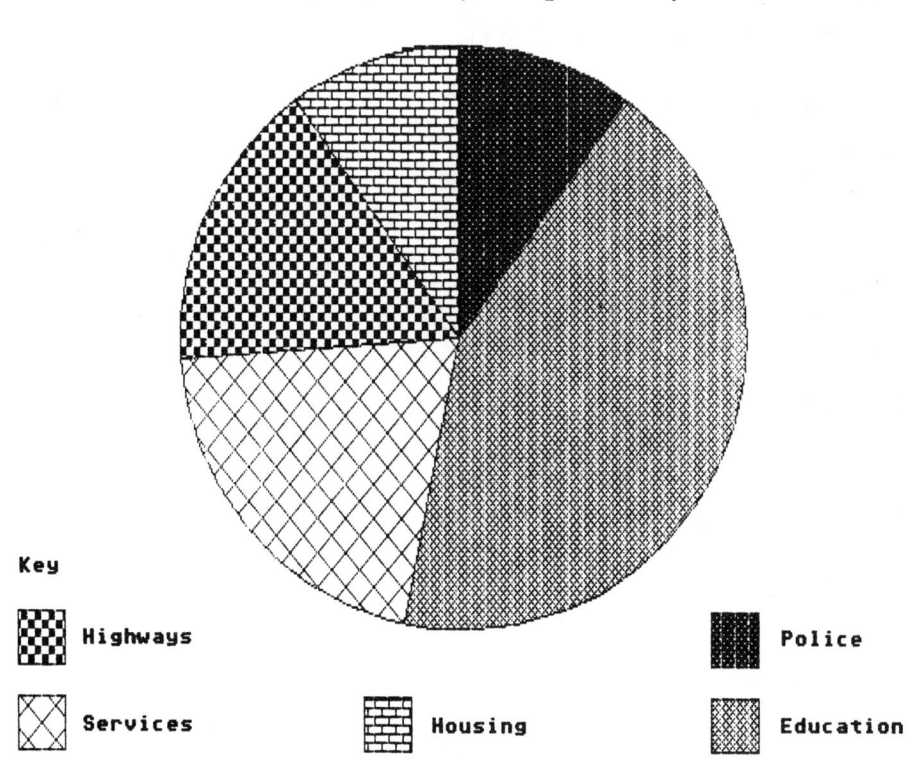

Figure 1.9

Question 27

On what was the most amount of money spent?

Question 28

Which *two* categories had the least amount of money spent on them?

Question 29

Is it possible to say how much money was spent on highways? Explain your answer.

Question 30

About what fraction (or percentage) of the council's money was spent on education?

The next set of questions is about the strip chart showing the results of our pets survey (Figure 1.10).

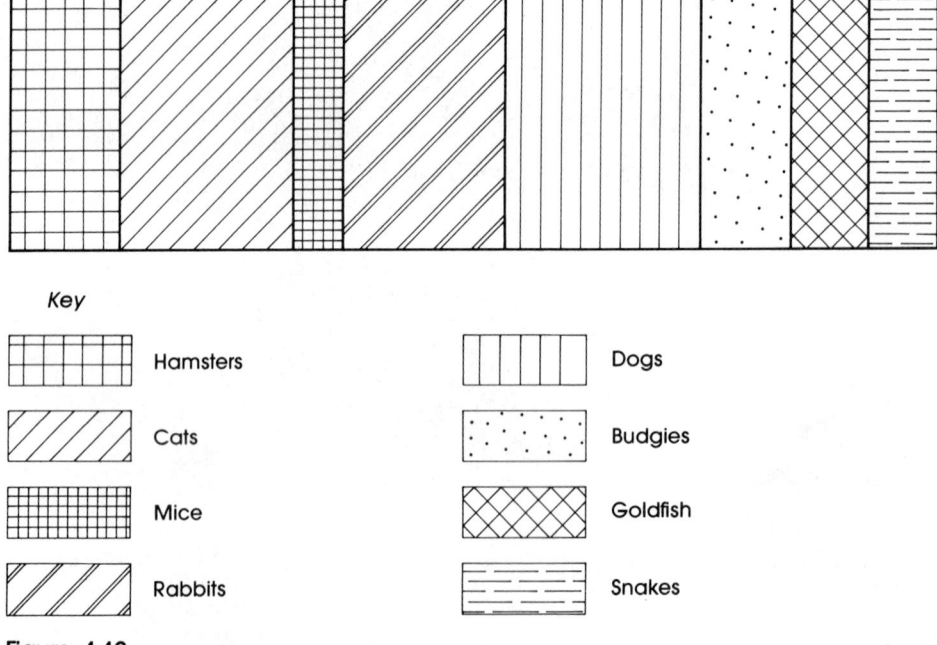

Figure 1.10

Question 31

Which pet would you say was the most popular and which the least?

Question 32

Could you say from the diagram *exactly* how many children preferred hamsters? Explain your answer.

Question 33

Write down an estimate for the number of people who said that budgies were their favourite pets.

Question 34

Write down the pets in order of popularity, starting with the most popular.

Finally, let's look at the pictogram which shows the results of our school meals survey (Figure 1.11). We asked 740 children to say which was the favourite bit of their school meal.

Pictogram to show results of survey of 740 children's favourite part of the school meal.

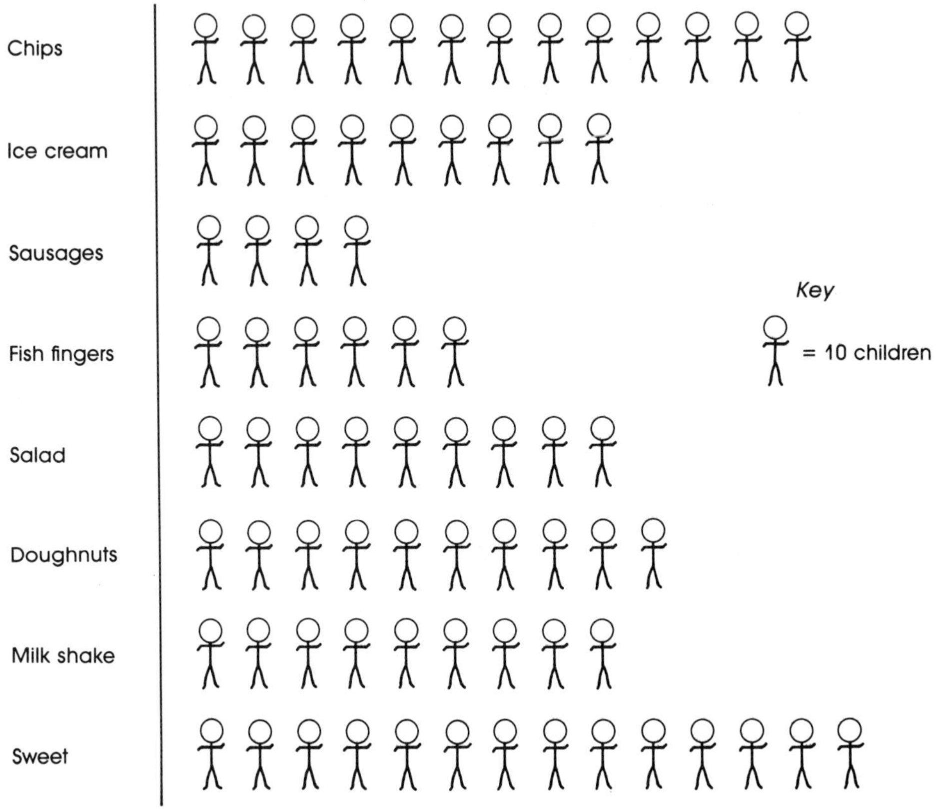

Food	Figures
Chips	12
Ice cream	9
Sausages	4
Fish fingers	6
Salad	8
Doughnuts	10
Milk shake	8
Sweet	13

Key: ⚫ = 10 children

Figure 1.11

Take careful note of the key as you answer these questions:

Question 35

How many children said that they preferred:

(a) Salad   (b) Chips   (c) Milk shake?

Question 36

How can you tell which is the most popular type of food? What is it? How many people said what their favourite was?

Question 37

The key says that each symbol equals 10 people. If you wanted to show 5 people how would you do it? How would you show 4 or 6? What do you think this tells you about pictograms?

Question 38

If we did our survey again in a bigger school of, say, 1500 pupils, what do you think would be a sensible scale to use?

DRAWING YOUR OWN DIAGRAMS

In Chapter 1 we saw that there are lots of different types of statistical diagrams and that the same information can be shown in different ways.

In this chapter, you will learn how to draw these diagrams and when to use each different type.

BAR CHARTS

One of the most popular types of diagram and one of the simplest to draw is the bar chart.

We did a small survey in a school and produced a bar chart to show the results.

We asked the 30 pupils in class 1T what they usually ate for breakfast. The answers, in the order the pupils gave them, are shown below.

1T Breakfast survey answers

Cereal	Drink only	Cereal
Cereal	Toast	Nothing
Nothing	Drink only	Toast
Toast	Cereal	Nothing
Drink only	Drink only	Cereal
Cereal	Nothing	Cereal
Cooked	Cereal	Nothing
Toast	Cooked	Toast
Toast	Nothing	Cooked
Nothing	Cereal	Cereal

To make the drawing of the bar chart easier, we first drew a tally chart. Below is a blank copy of the tally chart we used.

Breakfast	Tally	Freq.
Cereal Toast Cooked Nothing Drink only		
	Total	

ACTIVITY 1

Make a copy of this tally chart. Then complete it from the results of the survey in Table 2.1. Remember to use the five-bar gate system, like this ||||.

When you have finished the tally marks, fill in the frequency column at the end to show the total for each type of breakfast. Then fill in the total at the bottom and check that it comes to 30.

Now that the information is in this form we can draw the bar chart. There are several important things to remember when drawing a bar chart:

- All the bars should be the same width.
- The scale up the side should be clearly labelled.
- It should always have a title to say what it is about.
- The bars should be clearly labelled along the bottom.
- The diagram should be as neat and tidy as possible.
- It should be carefully shaded or coloured.

A copy of the bar chart we produced is shown on the next page. Using the totals in your tally chart, check that the bars are the correct height and that we have obeyed the rules given above.

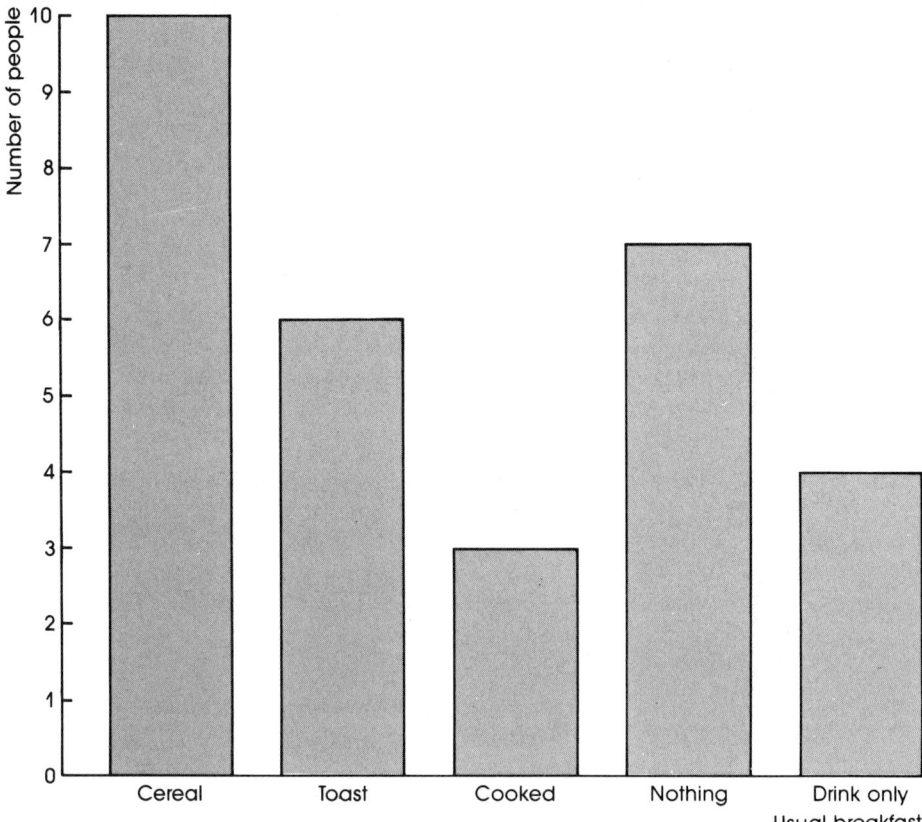

Figure 2.1

Now it's your turn

Now it's time for you to have a go. Remember to follow our rules carefully.

ACTIVITY 2

Do the breakfast survey in your class. From the information you get, draw up a tally chart and then produce a bar chart.

What will you do about the people who say that they sometimes have cereal and sometimes have toast? You can't count them twice!

You may have noticed that the bar chart we drew had gaps between the bars. Some bar charts do not; their bars are joined together. In the next activity you are asked to collect some more information and the bar chart you draw should have its bars joined together.

ACTIVITY 3

Ask all the members of your class how long it takes them to get to school in the morning. Use the following categories:

> 1–5 minutes (min) 16–20 min
> 6–10 min 21–25 min
> 11–15 min 26+ min

Draw up a tally chart for each range and then draw your bar chart, joining the bars together.

In which category would you put a person who says $5\frac{1}{2}$ minutes? The scale on the bottom of your bar chart should look like this.

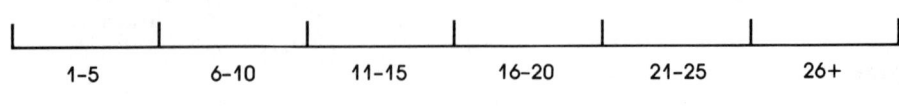

Figure 2.2

So what's the difference?

We have seen that some bar charts have gaps between their bars and others don't. So what's the difference?

Question 1

Write down *why* you think there is a difference. Discuss your answers with your friends and your teacher. For example, if you were drawing one bar chart of the heights of people in your class, and another of their favourite colours, which would have the gaps in it?

Question 2

Look at the following titles for bar charts and decide whether you would draw them with or without gaps:

(a) Types of pets owned by pupils in your class
(b) Heights of pupils in your class
(c) Distance in kilometres travelled to school by pupils in your class
(d) Makes of computer owned by pupils in your class
(e) Shoe sizes of pupils in your class

PICTOGRAMS

Another type of statistical diagram is the pictogram. Instead of using bars to show how many people are in each category, a pictogram uses small pictures or symbols. Below is a copy of the pictogram we saw in Chapter 1.

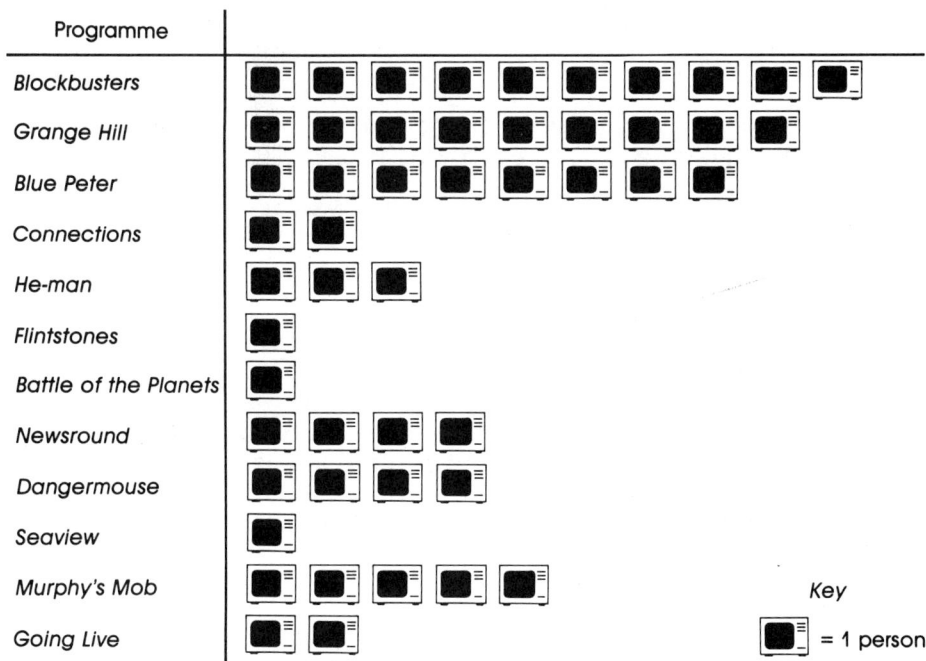

Pictogram to show children's favourite television programmes.

Figure 2.3

There are some important things to remember about pictograms.

- All the symbols should be the same.
- All the symbols should be the same size and arranged in neat rows and columns.
- The symbol used should have some connection with the subject of the pictogram.
- A pictogram must have a key to say what the symbol stands for.
- Like a bar chart, it should have a title.

Question 3

How many people liked *Dangermouse*?

Question 4

How many more people liked *Blue Peter* than *Seaview*?

Question 5

What would be a good symbol to use if you were drawing a pictogram on each of the following subjects?

(a) 1T breakfast survey
(b) A pets survey
(c) A computer survey

Question 6

If we surveyed the whole school in our breakfast survey, we might get up to 1000 answers. How many people should each symbol stand for then?

Question 7

Why would this make it unlikely that an exact reading could be taken from the pictogram?

ACTIVITY 4

Think of two more questions which you would like to ask your class. Make sure that they are ones for which you can easily record the results.

For each one, draw up a tally chart and then draw a pictogram, making sure that you take note of the points listed above.

For each of your diagrams, say why you chose the symbol and scale you did.

Question 8

Do you think that, for the last two questions you asked, the information would have been better shown in a pictogram or a bar chart? Explain your answer.

PIE CHARTS

Pie charts (or pie diagrams) are one of the most frequently used types of diagrams in statistics, but they are certainly not the easiest to draw!

The idea is simple: a circle (or pie) is cut up into sectors (or slices). Each slice is used to represent one group of the data. The size of each slice depends upon what fraction of the total each group is.

For example, in a survey, people were asked whether they would be willing to pay more for their daily newspaper, if it went up in price. One-half of the people interviewed said yes, one-quarter said no and the other quarter said they were not sure. So the Yes people are represented by half of the pie, those who said No get one-quarter and the Don't knows get the remaining quarter.

The pie chart is shown on the next page.

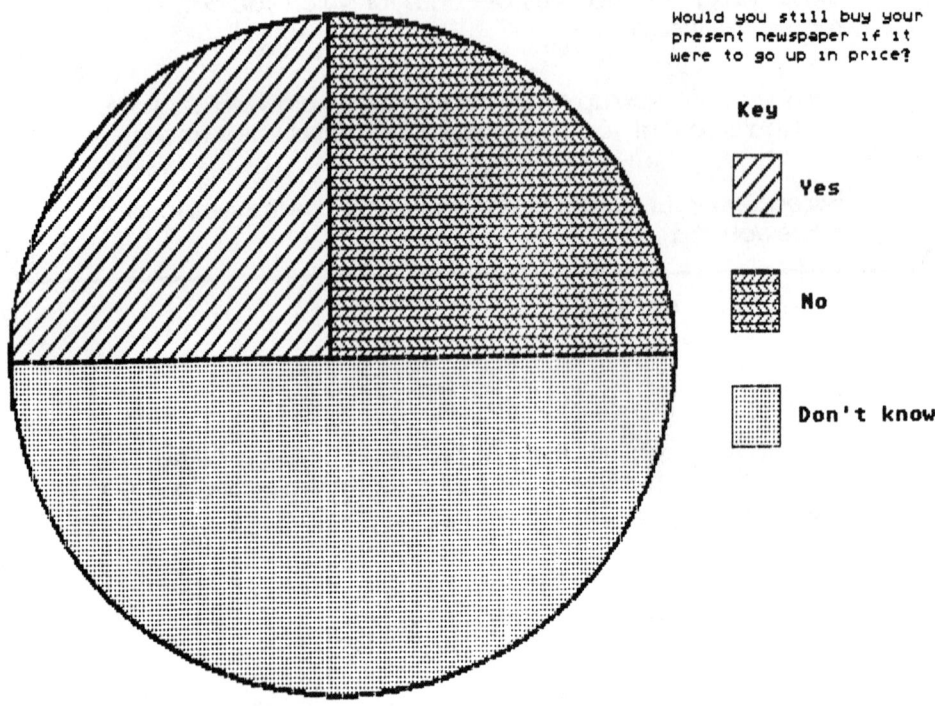

Figure 2.4

ACTIVITY 5

Draw pie charts to show the following survey data. Remember to shade or colour each diagram and give it a key and a title.

(a) In a survey asking which TV channel children watched the most, one-half said BBC 1, one-quarter said ITV and the other quarter were split equally between BBC 2 and Channel 4.

(b) A sample of 100 shoppers in a supermarket were asked what sort of butter or margarine they bought. One-quarter said butter, another quarter said sunflower margarine, a further quarter said ordinary margarine. The remainder was split equally between those who bought a slimming margarine and those who bought something different every time.

Of course, the more categories you have, or the more complicated the question is, the less likely it is that the answers will split into such nice easy fractions.

When this happens, we have to calculate how much of the pie to give to each group. To do this, we calculate what **angle** to draw in the circle. Remember that there are 360° in a full circle, so that if one group of people represents one-third of the total, it gets one-third of the 360° which is 120°, and so on for each group.

Here is an example which will make things clear:

We took the answers to our 1T breakfast survey, and drew a pie chart of their answers. Here are the calculations:

There are 30 people in the class and 360° in the circle, so each person in the class gets 360° ÷ 30 = 12°.

Having worked out that each person gets 12° of the pie, we then calculated how many degrees to give to each group of answers. We did this in the table below.

Answer	Total	Calculation	Angle
Cereal	10	10 × 12°	120°
Toast	6	6 × 12°	72°
Cooked	3	3 × 12°	36°
Nothing	7	7 × 12°	84°
Drink only	4	4 × 12°	48°
		Total	360°

To draw the pie chart, we drew the circle as before, marking the centre, and drew in the first line (see Figure 2.5, stage 1, on the next page).

We then measured the first angle (120°) from this line and drew in the next line. This is the 'cereal' slice (stage 2).

From this second line, we measured the next angle (72°) and drew in another line. This is the 'toast' slice (stage 3).

We continued this process until all the angles were drawn (stage 4).

The pie chart was then complete and ready to be coloured or shaded and have a key and title (stage 5).

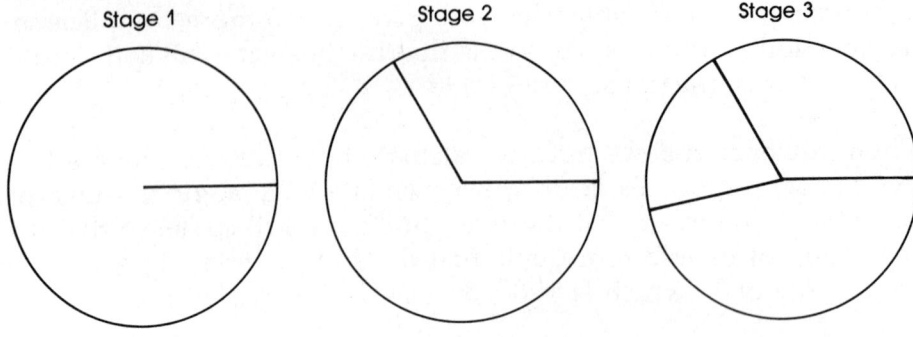

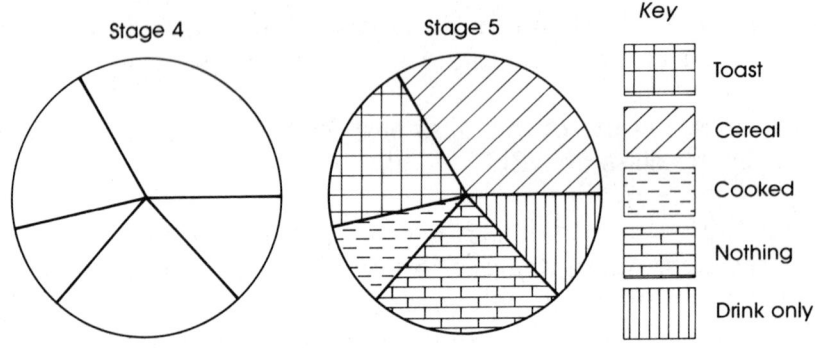

Pie chart to show results of 1T breakfast survey.

Figure 2.5

It is probably sensible to mark each sector in some way as you draw it, so that you do not forget which is which!

Question 9

Here are the total numbers of people questioned in various surveys. For each one calculate what angle in the pie chart each person would have.

(Remember that to do this, you divide 360° by the total number of people.)

(a) 45 people
(b) 24 people
(c) 60 people
(d) 120 people
(e) 100 people
(f) 32 people

Question 10

How are your answers to the last two parts of Question 9 different from the answers to the first four parts?

> **Discussion 1**
>
> Decide the best method of dealing with results like parts (e) and (f) in Question 9. Remember that a pie chart is not used to take exact readings, but for giving a general impression of size.
>
> At what point should you round off: when you first calculate the angle for each person, or when you have worked out the total angle for a particular group?

The next two activities give some data which you can use to practise drawing pie charts. Once you have done these, you will be ready to collect some data of your own (which might not produce nice round numbers!) and draw your own charts.

You will find it useful to have a calculator handy for this work.

ACTIVITY 6

We surveyed 45 teachers and asked them which newspaper they usually bought. Here are the results.

Guardian	15
Independent	9
Mirror	7
Mail	6
Express	5
None	3

(Remember, the angle for each person is 360° ÷ 45.)

Complete a table as we did in the example and then draw a pie chart.

ACTIVITY 7

During the 30 days of June last year we recorded how many hours of sunshine there were on each day. The results are shown in the table below.

Hours of sunshine	Number of days with that number of hours' sunshine
Less than 3	4
3	5
4	2
5	6
6	4
7	3
8	4
More than 8	2

Draw a pie chart to show these data.

ACTIVITY 8

Either take the information which you gathered to draw your pictograms in Activity 4, or ask your class another two questions. Use the data to produce two pie charts. It is likely that you will get a decimal number when you calculate the angle, so be careful.

STEM AND LEAF PLOTS

A stem and leaf plot is an easy way of showing data. It is often used for displaying measurements, especially if decimals are involved.

The technique is best described with an example. Let's return to class 1T! This time we asked them to measure each other's height using a height chart on the wall. The results are shown on the next page (all results are given to the nearest centimetre).

141	153	156
142	147	170
162	145	159
158	144	163
167	171	141
146	156	150
160	151	153
169	161	149
147	153	137
160	155	145

The **stem** of the number in this case would be the first two digits (the hundreds and the tens) and the **leaf** is the last number (the units).

To draw the stem and leaf plot, we make a list of all the stems and then write the leaves next to each one. The result looks like this.

Heights of class 1T members (cm)

```
13   7
14   1 1 2 4 5 5 6 7 7 9
15   0 1 3 3 3 5 6 6 8 9
16   0 0 1 2 3 7 9
17   0 1
```

Not only does this show the number of heights in each category (e.g. 130–139 cm, 140–149 cm, etc.), but also still shows the original data, which a bar chart would not.

Question 11

Why would it be easy to find the middle value when the data were shown in a stem and leaf plot?

Question 12

Which other 'special' values would be easier to find once the data was displayed in this way?

If there were a lot of data, it might be easier to split them in to groups of 5 rather than 10. To do this, you would use the same stem twice but group different leaves to each one.

This was done with the 1T height survey, as shown below.

Heights of class 1T members (cm)

```
13   7
14   1 1 2 4
14   5 5 6 7 7 9
15   0 1 3 3 3
15   5 6 6 8 9
16   0 0 1 2 3
16   7 9
17   0 1
```

Note that the stems and the leaves on them are in order of size. You might like to make a rough copy first, to make sure you get this right.

ACTIVITY 9

At the end of term, 1T did a small maths test and were given a percentage (that is a mark out of 100). Below are their results.

24	56	83
45	68	53
35	70	73
65	74	51
49	91	29
54	52	89
48	57	63
69	44	66
96	81	57
58	68	77

Use these results to produce a stem and leaf plot.

ACTIVITY 10

After getting their heights and test results, we next weighed members of 1T! Their weights in kg are shown below. Use these results to produce a stem and leaf plot. Because the weights are very similar, you might think that it is a good idea to use the double stem method described earlier.

45	53	57
43	49	56
63	41	53
57	59	60
54	50	47
56	59	49
47	40	64
60	53	51
42	49	55
56	62	57

Discussion 2

How do you think a stem and leaf plot works when you are using decimal numbers?

For example, if you measure the length of everyone's little finger, most of the measurements would not be a whole number of centimetres — they would involve decimals.

Which bit of the number would form the stem and which the leaf?

ACTIVITY 11

Take some measurements in your own class and use them to produce stem and leaf plots.

You could measure heights and weights, or use some of your own test results if you have done one recently. Better still, you could think of some ideas of your own. For example, you could measure hand spans, or the time it takes people to perform a certain task, such as writing 100 words or running 100 metres.

TO SUM UP

We have looked in detail at four of the most common types of statistical diagrams. There are lots of others, some of which are quite a bit more complicated, and you will see them in later chapters.

There are also some variations on the ones we have already looked at. For example, a **line chart** is a type of bar chart, where the bars are replaced by simple straight lines. Again, it is the height of the line which gives the number of items in each group. A line chart is sometimes also drawn horizontally, rather like a pictogram, instead of vertically, like a bar chart. Figure 2.6 is an example. You might like to try something like this in Activity 12.

Most charts can be drawn so that they appear to be three dimensional. This does not alter the way the chart shows the data, but it can make it look much better. Three-dimensional charts are

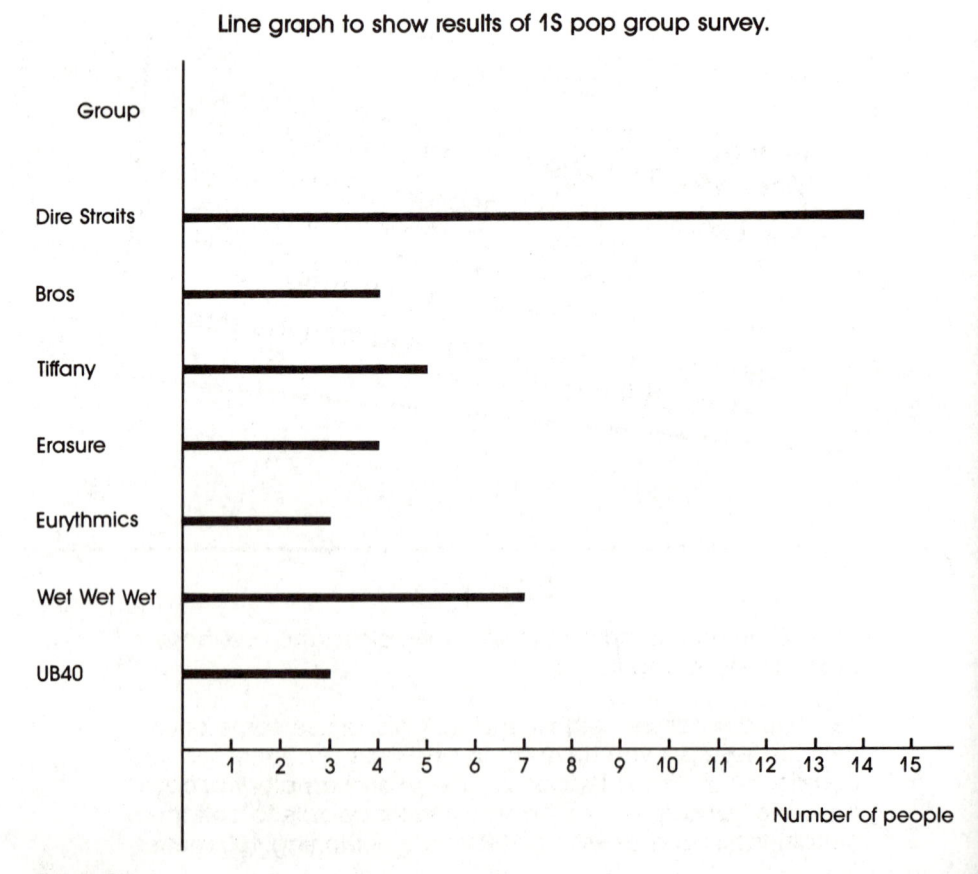

Line graph to show results of 1S pop group survey.

Group

Dire Straits

Bros

Tiffany

Erasure

Eurythmics

Wet Wet Wet

UB40

1 2 3 4 5 6 7 8 9 10 11 12 13 14 15

Number of people

Figure 2.6

often used on television news, where powerful computers can be used to produce the graphics. Watch out for them next time you are watching the news. We have done this with the 1T breakfast survey.

Three-dimensional bar chart to show results of 1T breakfast survey.

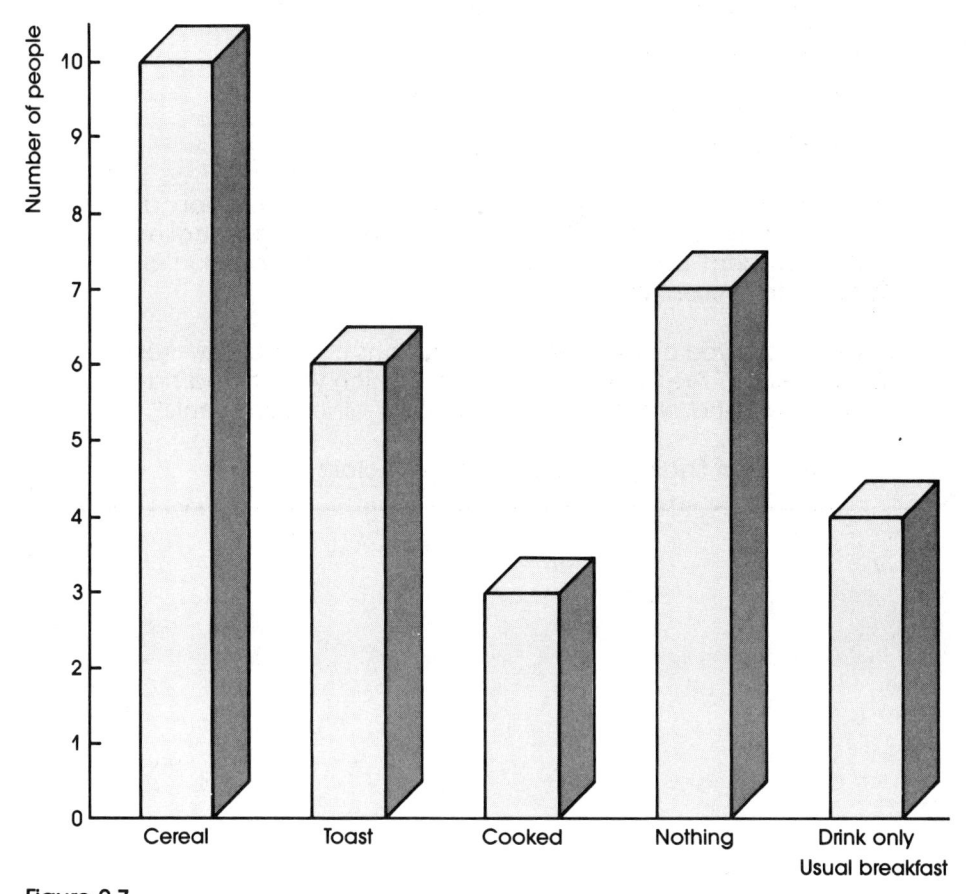

Number of people vs *Usual breakfast*: Cereal 10, Toast 6, Cooked 3, Nothing 7, Drink only 4.

Figure 2.7

The most important thing is to be able to use the correct chart at the correct time. This means that you really have to think about the data you have collected before you start drawing your diagrams.

In Activity 12, there is a little class project. It will involve you in collecting some more data of your own, but this time you will not be told which diagrams to draw. It will be up to you, and your friends working with you, to decide which to use when. Discuss it carefully, and agree which you are going to use.

ACTIVITY 12

You are going to compare a national newspaper with a local one. How? Well, that is for you to decide! Some ideas might be:

- What sort of adverts do they have?
- What sort of stories do they have? How many?
- How much space do they give to various things?
- How many people buy each one?
- Think up some ideas of your own.

Split into groups and decide what measurements you are going to take and what statistics you are going to collect. Collect them between you and then decide how you are going to present them.

What have you proved? What conclusions can you draw from your results? Are there some statistics which you should have collected and didn't? Do you have any other comments?

Present your findings to the rest of your class.

3 AVERAGES AND RANGES

AVERAGES

You must have heard the word **average** used lots of times on television, or seen it in newspaper headlines like the ones at the top of this page. Have you ever wondered what it means?

> **Discussion 1**
>
> What do you think the word average means?
>
> Try to make up some sentences which have the word average in them.
>
> Have they got anything in common?

There are several different ways to work out the average of a set of data.

Here is an example which might help to explain one of them.

Classes 2G and 2H are collecting money for a charity appeal on television. They both organise lots of sponsored events and they both want to be the class which collects the most money.

At the end of the time allowed, each class adds up all the money to see who has collected the most. They have both done very well! Class 2G has a total of £364, while 2H has £375.

Class 2H are celebrating the fact that they have got the most money when Stephen, a pupil in 2G, comes in and says 'This isn't fair! You were bound to collect more money than us because there are more of you!'

> **Discussion 2**
>
> Why does the size of the class make a difference to the result of the competition?
>
> What do you think the pupils should do to get a fair result?

After a heated discussion, they all realise that because 2G has 28 members while 2H has 30, it isn't really fair just to look at the total each class has collected.

Anne, a member of 2H, suggests that each class should divide its money up equally between all its members, as if each pupil in the class had collected the same amount. They would then be able to tell which class had done best.

Here are the calculations which helped them do this.

Class 2G:
£364 ÷ 28 pupils = £13 per pupil

Class 2H:
£375 ÷ 30 pupils = £12.50 per pupil

> **Discussion 3**
>
> Which class do you think has done the best?
>
> Is it fair to divide up the money in this way?

The figures £13 per pupil and £12.50 per pupil are called the **mean** amount collected. It is one way of working out an average.

In fact, all the classes in the second year are collecting money for the same appeal.

ACTIVITY 1

Here are the details for each of the other second year classes in the school. For each class, calculate the **mean** amount of money collected.

> 2J £283.50 from 27 pupils
> 2K £354.00 from 24 pupils
> 2L £359.60 from 29 pupils
> 2M £358.80 from 26 pupils

Calculate the mean amount collected by each pupil in the year as a whole (that is the total amount of money collected, divided by the total number of pupils). (Don't forget 2G and 2H!) What does this figure represent?

The second-year classes were also involved in the school's athletics programme. Every member of the year has to run the 100 m race. Here are the results for some of the boys in 2G.

> Stephen 13.9 seconds (s)
> Nick   14.2 s
> David   16.1 s
> John   15.6 s
> Ian   14.9 s
> Tom   15.3 s

Question 1

Find the mean time taken to run 100 m by these boys. (Remember, you will have to calculate the total of the times first!)

Question 2

Karl took 15.9 s to finish the race. If we included his time in the calculation, would the mean time be larger or smaller? Why?

Of course, the girls took part in the race as well. Here are some of their times.

Claire	14.7 s
Cathy	15.7 s
Barbara	15.8 s
Alison	14.5 s
Julie	14.3 s

Question 3

Calculate the mean time for these girls.

Question 4

Is the average smaller or larger than that of the boys? Would you have been able to tell this just by looking at the numbers?

WHAT'S YOUR AVERAGE?

Now it's over to you! Next you will calculate some averages from data you have collected yourself. Of course, they may not come out with nice whole numbers, but if you use a calculator (or you are good at dividing) this should not matter!

ACTIVITY 2

Collect some data from your own class, for example

- Heights
- Weights
- Test/exam scores
- Pocket money
- Times to complete a certain task — you could have a race at lunch-time!
- Your own ideas

You may like to split some groups up into girls and boys, and calculate the averages separately and then as a whole group, so that you can compare them.

When you are doing the calculations, make sure you show your working carefully in your book, even if you are using your calculator.

Discuss your results.

SHOWING THE MEAN ON A DIAGRAM

Figure 3.1 is a bar chart showing the hours of sunshine for each month last year. The line across the bar chart shows the mean hours of sunshine over the year.

Bar chart to show hours of sunshine each month last year.

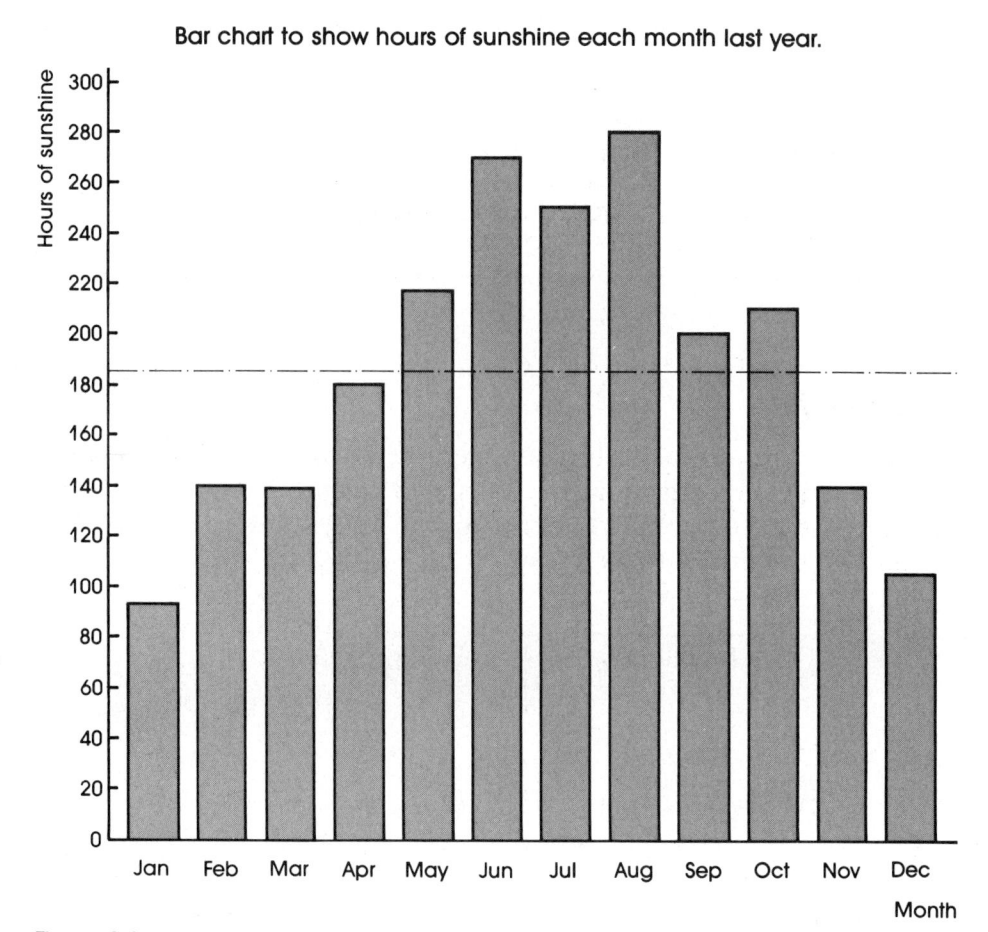

Figure 3.1

Here's the calculation.

    Total = 93 + 140 + 139 + 180 + 217 + 270 + 250 + 280 + 200 + 210 + 140 + 106

           = 2225

    Mean = 2225 ÷ 12

           = 185.4 hours per month

Question 5

What can you say about the heights of the bars above the line compared with the gaps underneath it? Why does this happen?

ACTIVITY 3

Choose an appropriate set of results from Activity 2 and draw a bar chart for them. It will have to be a set of data which has not been grouped together as 1-10, 11-20, etc. Check with your teacher before you start. Draw the line which represents the mean. Does the same thing happen as before?

Grouped data

Data is often much easier to use when it has been put into **groups**, but this makes it slightly more difficult to calculate the mean. For example, we asked some children how many pets they each had at home. The results were as follows.

Number of pets	Number of children
0	24
1	32
2	18
3	8
4	6
5	2
6	1

Before we can calculate the mean number of pets, we must work out how many pets there are altogether.

The first 24 children had no pets, the next 32 had 1 pet (32 so far), the next 18 had 2 pets (that's 36, so 68 so far), and so on.

There are 132 pets altogether, and 91 children. To calculate the mean we divide 132 by 91, giving 1.45 pets per person on average. If you think that's a funny number of pets to have then read the next section! But before you do that, try these activities.

ACTIVITY 4

During a particularly good August, we recorded the number of hours of sunshine in a seaside resort. The results are given here.

Hours of sunshine	Number of days
5	8
6	9
7	6
8	4
9	2
10	2

Calculate the mean number of hours of sunshine during this month.

ACTIVITY 5

A tissue manufacturer labelled its boxes 'Average contents 100 tissues'. A sample of 200 boxes was taken and the following results obtained.

Number of tissues	Number of boxes
197	36
198	42
199	23
200	52
201	28
202	19

Calculate the mean number of tissues in a box in this sample.

What other sorts of average are there?

ACTIVITY 6

Collect the shoe sizes of everyone in your class. Calculate the mean in the usual way.

Question 6

Think carefully about the mean shoe size. Does anyone actually wear that size of shoe?

You may well have got a decimal as the average. If you didn't, you were lucky. Try adding in your teacher's shoe size and see what happens to your average!

In this case, the mean is not a very useful number, because it often comes out as an impossible size which nobody wears.

Instead, you can use different ways to work out an average.

THE MEDIAN

An average is sometimes described as a number somewhere in the middle of a set of data. That's exactly what the **median** is. It's the middle number of your set of data. Of course, you must make sure that your data are in order from smallest to largest first. It wouldn't make much sense just to find the middle one if the data were still in the order you first wrote down — you might get the smallest value!

ACTIVITY 7

Here are the results of some shoe-size surveys from classes 2J and 2L. For each one, find the median, by first putting the numbers in size order, starting with the smallest.

Class 2J:

```
6  8  6  9  4  5  10  6   5
7  6  7  4  4  3   9  11  6
3  5  6  7  8  8   5   8  8
```

Class 2L:

```
5  4  6  7   8  3  5   6  10
7  8  6  5  11  5  7   8   9
4  5  8  7   5  3  6  10   7
6  7
```

Question 7

Do you think this is a better way of working out this sort of average? Give your reasons.

What about class 2G?

Here are the results of the same survey with class 2G.

Class 2G:

6 8 5 4 7 9 4 3 2
5 6 7 6 5 3 8 9 2
4 5 8 9 5 4 6 7 8
5

ACTIVITY 8

Work out the median of the 2G data.

Describe any problem you have found.

How do you think you could get around this problem?

When trying to find the median of an even number of numbers like this, you always find there are *two* numbers in the middle. The way to deal with this is to find the number in the middle of the two numbers, or in other words to find their mean!

In the case of class 2G the two middle numbers are 5 and 6, so the median is 5.5.

ACTIVITY 9

Use this method to find the median of this set of shoe-size data from class 2H.

5 4 6 7 8 9 2 4 5
6 10 3 5 4 6 2 7 8
3 4 5 8 7 3 5 8 11
6 7 5

Question 8

What problem do you come across again when calculating the average this way?

Finding the median from a diagram

One of the easiest diagrams from which to find the median is a stem and leaf plot.

Question 9

What is it about a stem and leaf plot that makes finding the median so easy?

ACTIVITY 10

Take one of your sets of data from Activity 2. The pocket money survey might be a good choice. Draw a stem and leaf plot from your data. Then find and mark the median value.

Question 10

Describe as carefully as you can where the median is on your diagram, and how many numbers there are either side of it.

THE MODE

The third and final method for calculating the average of a set of data is also the simplest!

The **mode** of a set of data (sometimes called the modal value) is simply the one which occurs most often or is the most popular. This guarantees that we do not get a silly answer with surveys like the shoe size ones.

ACTIVITY 11

Go back through the four shoe-size surveys and your own, and work out the mode in each case.

ACTIVITY 12

Make a list of all the different types of statistical diagrams you can think of. For each one, say how you would be able to find the mode. Which do you think would be the easiest?

By the way, if two things are equally popular, or occur an equal number of times, they are *both* said to be the mode. You should not average them as you did with the median.

ACTIVITY 13

In this activity, there are some example sets of data. For each one work out the average in the three different ways you have seen in this chapter. You should then say, giving reasons, which version of the average is the best in each case. When you have finished, discuss your answers with your group or class.

(a) We went into a factory and asked 20 people at random how much they earned in a week. These are the results.

£120 £120 £110 £130 £250 £110 £90
£115 £113 £550 £120 £130 £115 £105
£90   £120 £115 £95   £550 £120

(b) These are the monthly rainfall figures for 1988.

150 mm 140 mm 145 mm 102 mm 88 mm   50 mm
45 mm   58 mm   85 mm   100 mm 96 mm   130 mm

(c) These are 30 totals gained from throwing 2 dice together in a board game.

7 8 5 7 9 5 2 10 6 5
6 9 11 5 7 8 7 9   12 4
5 7 4 6 8 9 7 2   10 7

(d) These are the number of books sold in a bookshop over a period of 12 weeks.

851 743   268 980 576 863
758 1203 754 698 465 921

(e) These are the prices of 15 similar 3-bedroomed houses in northern England.

£45 000 £48 850 £53 000 £62 250 £54 500
£39 950 £47 750 £61 000 £39 150 £34 900
£43 000 £56 350 £54 100 £61 250 £55 550

(f) These are the numbers of chocolate buttons found in 20 randomly selected packets.

36 35 36 40 38 39 34 39 41 37
38 37 40 39 33 36 40 38 36 35

ACTIVITY 14

Go back to the data you collected in Activity 2 to calculate means. For each set, calculate the median and mode and say whether you think these are better averages than the mean.

DOES THE AVERAGE TELL IT ALL?

Try the following activity.

ACTIVITY 15

Look at the following two sets of data for hours of sunshine during the year in two different countries.

Month	Set 1	Set 2
Jan	154	50
Feb	161	80
Mar	165	120
Apr	170	165
May	173	190
Jun	185	236
Jul	190	260
Aug	198	301
Sep	187	276
Oct	164	197
Nov	153	101
Dec	140	64

Work out the mean hours of sunshine in each place and draw a bar chart for each.

You should have found that the two means are exactly the same. Now look carefully at the two bar charts.

Question 11

Describe the main differences between the two bar charts you have drawn. Where do you think each place is?

Question 12

Explain why the mean by itself is not enough to describe the data.

RANGES

The **range** of a set of data is a simple calculation that helps get around the problem in question 12.

The range is the gap or difference between the smallest and largest numbers in the data. For example, in set 1 of the sunshine figures, the smallest number is 140 and the largest number is 198, so the range is:

$$198 - 140 = 58 \text{ hours}$$

Question 13

Work out the range for set 2 of the sunshine data.

Question 14

Say how the mean and range, used together, would help someone who hasn't seen the data get a better idea of what it is like.

Question 15

Look at the two pictograms in Figure 3.2.

Which of them shows the set of data with the greatest range? How can you tell?

(a) Pictogram to show 2Z test scores (%) in science.

(b) Pictogram to show 2Z test scores (%) in maths.

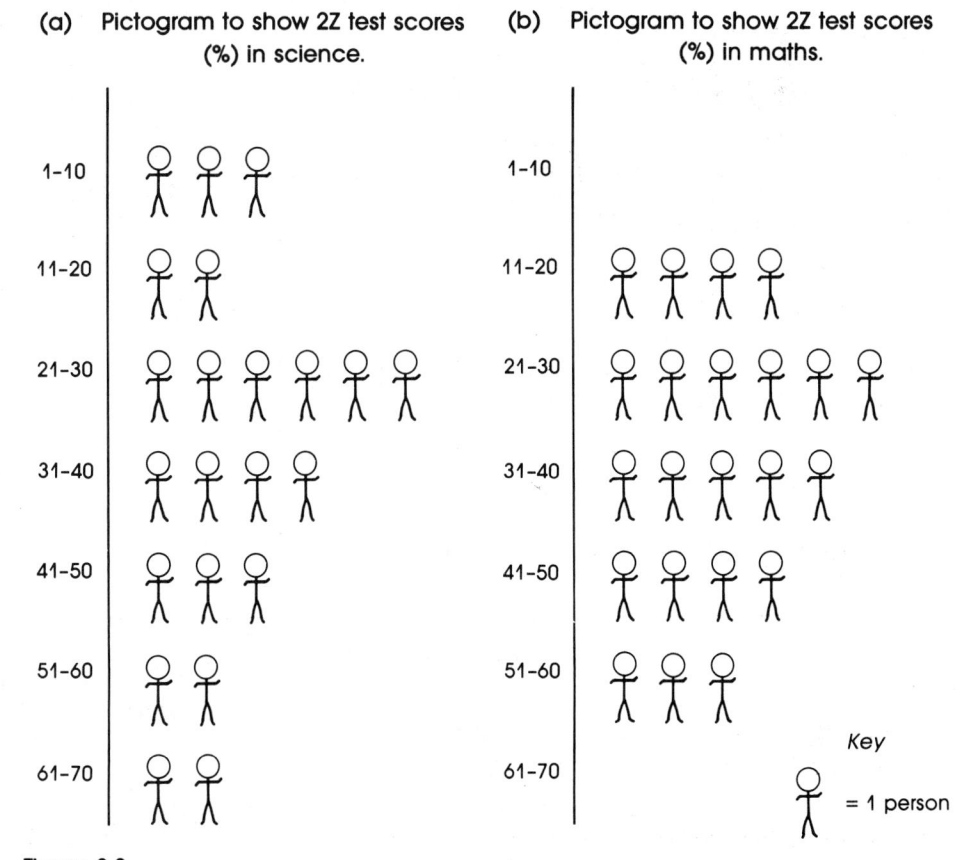

Score	Science	Maths
1–10	3	
11–20	2	4
21–30	6	6
31–40	4	5
41–50	3	4
51–60	2	3
61–70	2	

Key: 👤 = 1 person

Figure 3.2

Question 16

Look at the stem and leaf plots below. Which shows the data with the greatest range? How can you tell?

Stem and leaf plot to show 2Z test scores (%) in French						Stem and leaf plot to show 2Z test scores (%) in German					
1	2	4	7			1					
2	0	6	8	8		2	1	4	7		
3	1	4	9	9		3	2	6	8		
4	3	5	7			4	1	3	7	9	
5	2	2	5	6	9	5	3	5	6	8	9
6	6	9				6	7	8	8		
7	5					7	0	3			
8						8	2				
9						9	4				

Let's look at another use for this sort of calculation. We tested the *response times* of two different taxi firms. The response time is the time taken for the taxi to reach a customer, once it had been requested. The figures are given in minutes.

Here are some of the results from the two firms.

Carol's Cars	Alan's Autos
12	14
15	12
9	11
17	14
8	12
13	10
16	13
19	12
10	13
7	14
13	14

ACTIVITY 16

Choose a suitable type of diagram to display the data above and draw one for each set.

Calculate the mean and the range for each company. (You may need a calculator.)

Question 17

How many times did each company take more than 14 minutes to answer a call?

Question 18

How many times did each company take less than 11 minutes to answer a call?

Question 19

If you had an important meeting to get to within 30 minutes and you knew the journey would take 15 minutes, which company would you call to make *sure* of getting there? Why?

Question 20

If you had to attend the same meeting, but you would like at least the *chance* of a quick cup of coffee before it started, which company would you call? Why? What might the result be?

SOME EXPERIMENTS TO TRY

ACTIVITY 17

Take two ordinary dice numbered 1 to 6. You are going to throw them together and add the scores to get the total. Keep throwing the dice until you score 11. Write down how many goes it takes you to score 11. Do this 10 times. Find the mean, median and mode of the number of shakes it takes you to score 11. Also, find the range of the data. Collect all the results for your class and find the averages and range for all the data. Discuss your results. If you wish, present your results with a diagram.

ACTIVITY 18

Repeat Activity 17, using 7 as your target score instead of 11. Again, collect together the class results. Discuss the differences between the two sets of results. Which average is the best to use in this case? How does the range help you explain what is going on? Try to find the reason for the difference in your two sets of results.

ACTIVITY 19

You can try a similar experiment to those described in the previous activities with a game of Snap. Simply record the number of goes it takes you before one of the players says Snap!

To finish this chapter, there is another short piece of project work. It is best to do this in groups, and of course it must be well planned. Decide *exactly* what you are going to do and what statistics you need to collect before you put pen to paper!

ACTIVITY 20

For this project, you will collect some statistics and then present a short report on your findings. Your report must concentrate on calculating appropriate averages and ranges and using them to explain your findings.

You could simply collect statistics from members of your class, or from other pupils in the school, or you could even go outside to collect your data. For example, you could collect data about traffic flow near your school or in your town, or you could look at the prices of houses in your area.

4 THE TRUTH, THE WHOLE TRUTH, AND NOTHING BUT THE TRUTH?

Look at the two diagrams in Figure 4.1. The first was prepared by a record company which specialises in producing singles. The second was prepared by a different company specialising in selling LPs containing lots of chart hits.

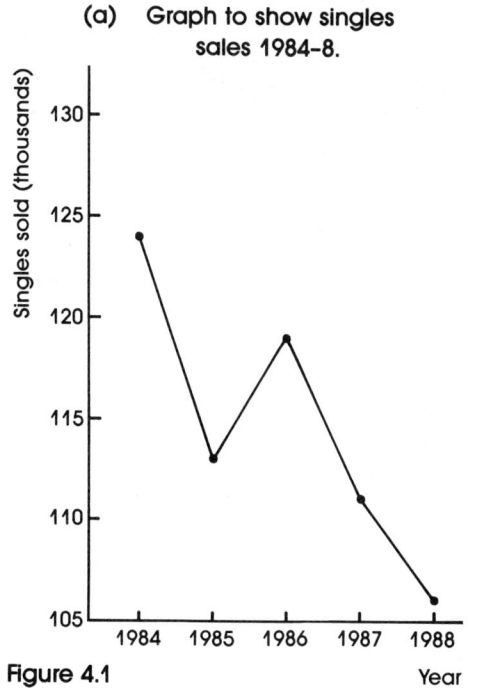

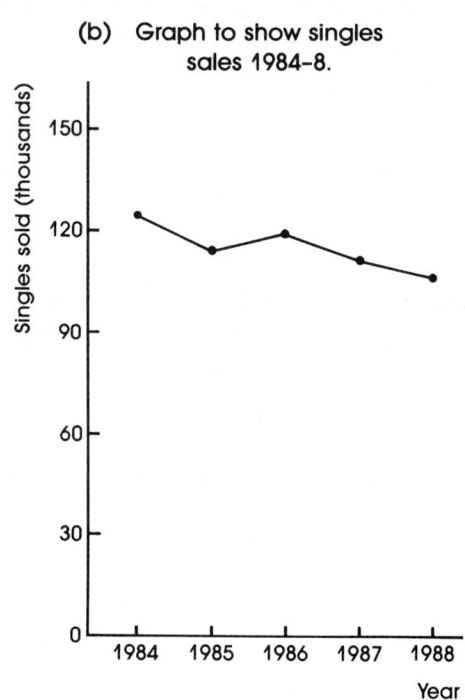

(a) Graph to show singles sales 1984-8.

(b) Graph to show singles sales 1984-8.

Figure 4.1

ACTIVITY 1

Look carefully at the two graphs in Figure 4.1 and how they differ from each other. You can be sure that the *facts* in each of them are correct.

(a) Do the graphs show the same information?

(b) What is it that makes them look so different?

(c) Is this way of changing the graph dishonest?

(d) Which graph do you think is the fairer?

(e) Try to explain *why* each company would want to display the information in the way that they have.

This is one way of changing a graph to make a point or to alter the way it looks. The second graph looks much more dramatic than the first, but it displays the same basic information. It is not lying, but is it telling the whole truth?

In this chapter you will have to look at all the diagrams very carefully to spot all the tricks! Remember this when you are doing the next activity and try to put yourself in the place of the people described.

ACTIVITY 2

On the following pages are three pairs of diagrams. Each pair shows the same information, but as in Figure 4.1, they look rather different! Read the explanation which goes with each one and say which graph would be used by which person and why.

Look carefully at the scale on each graph, because you will soon be doing some graphs of your own, and you will get some hints from these examples.

(a) Graph to show car sales over an eight-month period.

(b) Graph to show car sales over an eight-month period.

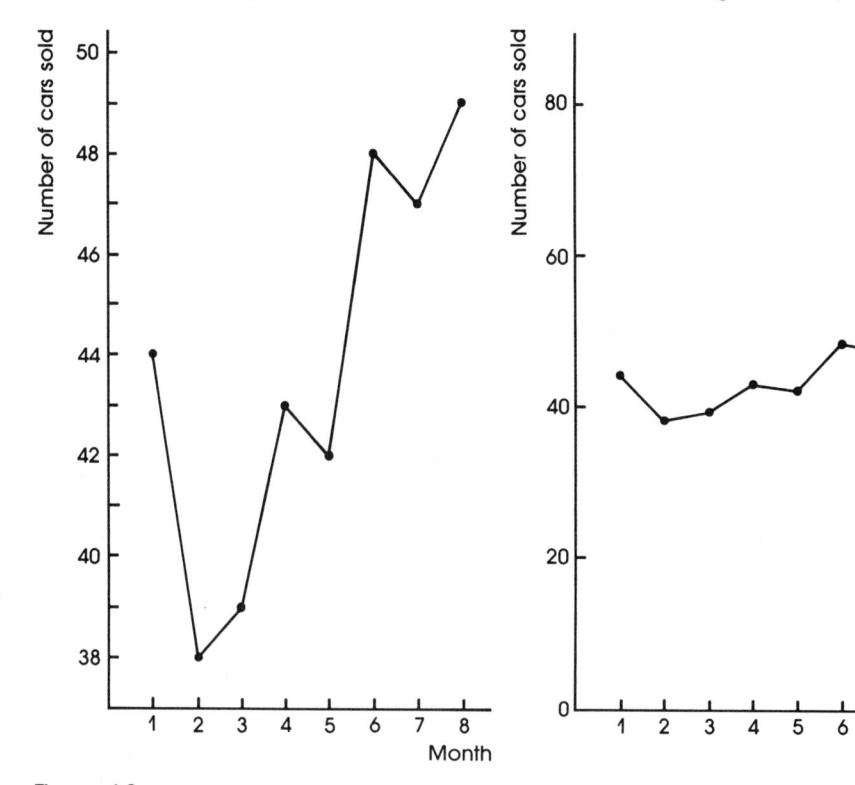

Figure 4.2

(a) A car sales manager is trying to prove to one of the sales staff that his sales figures are not increasing enough so he is in danger of losing his job. The salesperson is trying to show that he is doing well. Which graph in Figure 4.2 would each choose and why?

(b) The government is trying to prove to the voters that it is managing to hold unemployment at a steady level. The opposition, on the other hand, wants to show that unemployment is rising steeply. Which graph in Figure 4.3 would each choose and why?

(c) A new DJ has taken over the breakfast show on a local radio station and wants to show that the audience figures have gone up. The station manager, however, is not impressed! She thinks that the new DJ is not doing a good job and means to prove it. Which graph in Figure 4.4 would each choose and why?

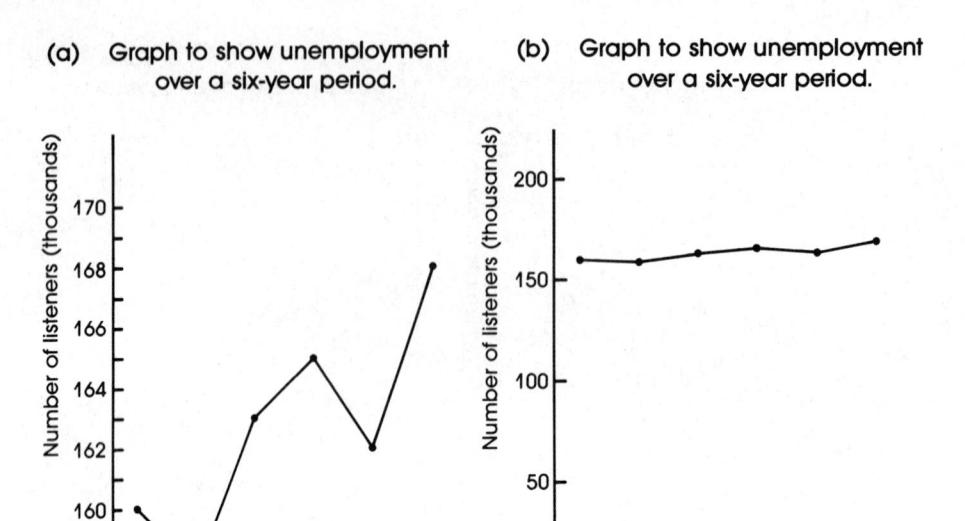

(a) Graph to show unemployment over a six-year period.

(b) Graph to show unemployment over a six-year period.

Figure 4.3

(a) Graph to show the number of listeners to the breakfast show, January to June.

(a) Graph to show the number of listeners to the breakfast show, January to June.

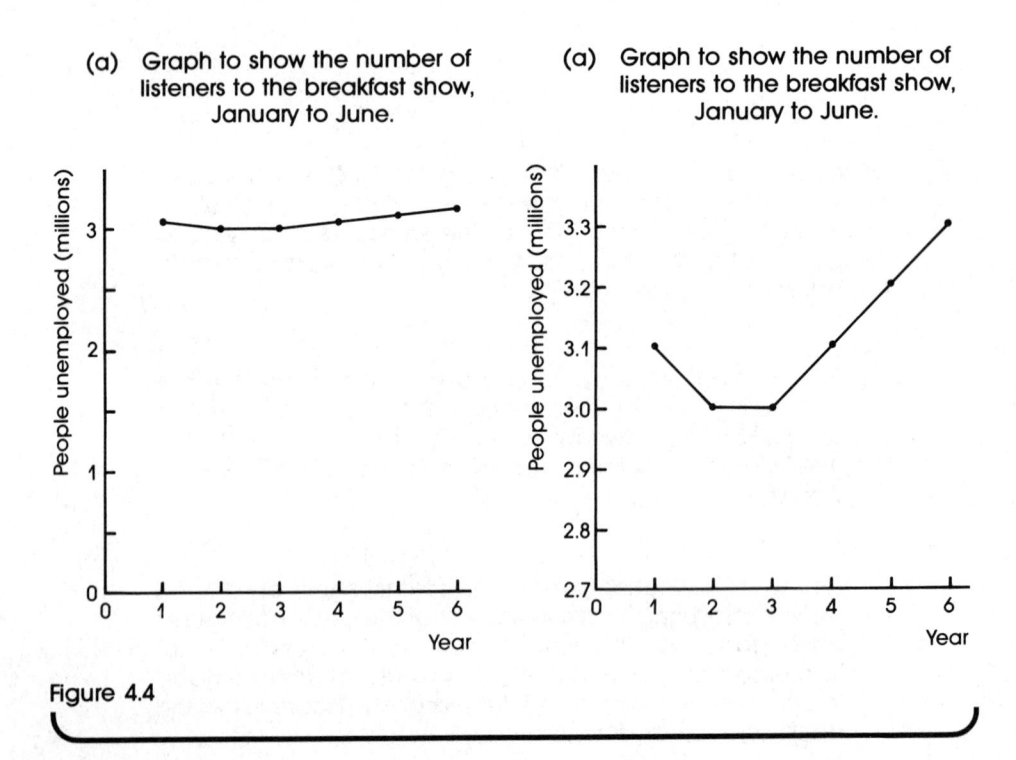

Figure 4.4

ACTIVITY 3

Now here are some more situations for you to think about. This time, you are provided with the data and asked to produce two graphs, one to fit each situation in each case.

(a) The audience figures for a theatre over a period of eight weeks are shown below. The person in charge of the box office is anxious to show that the audiences are increasing dramatically because he wants some extra staff. The manager doesn't want to pay any more staff and so wants to show that the audiences are remaining fairly steady. Draw one graph for each person.

Week 1	1960	Week 5	2005
Week 2	1985	Week 6	2040
Week 3	1980	Week 7	2045
Week 4	2010	Week 8	2060

(b) The number of cars passing through a small village on an average day over a six-year period is shown below. The villagers want the traffic to be diverted, whereas the county council does not want to spend any money on such a scheme. Draw one graph for each.

1983	780
1984	820
1985	810
1986	830
1987	850
1988	860

(c) A publishing company launched a new women's magazine for a six-month trial. At the end of the trial period the editor and staff want to keep the magazine going but the publishers are not so sure. Shown below are the sales figures for the six month trial period. Draw one graph for each.

Month 1	320 000
Month 2	290 000
Month 3	295 000
Month 4	305 000
Month 5	300 000
Month 6	298 000

ADVERTISING

It is not just graphs that can have different scales. Diagrams such as bar charts and pictograms can be altered as well.

ACTIVITY 4

Every six months, a bank announces its profits. It wants to show that it is doing very well, so it produces the following bar chart showing profits for the last two years.

Bar chart to show a bank's net profits over a two-year period.

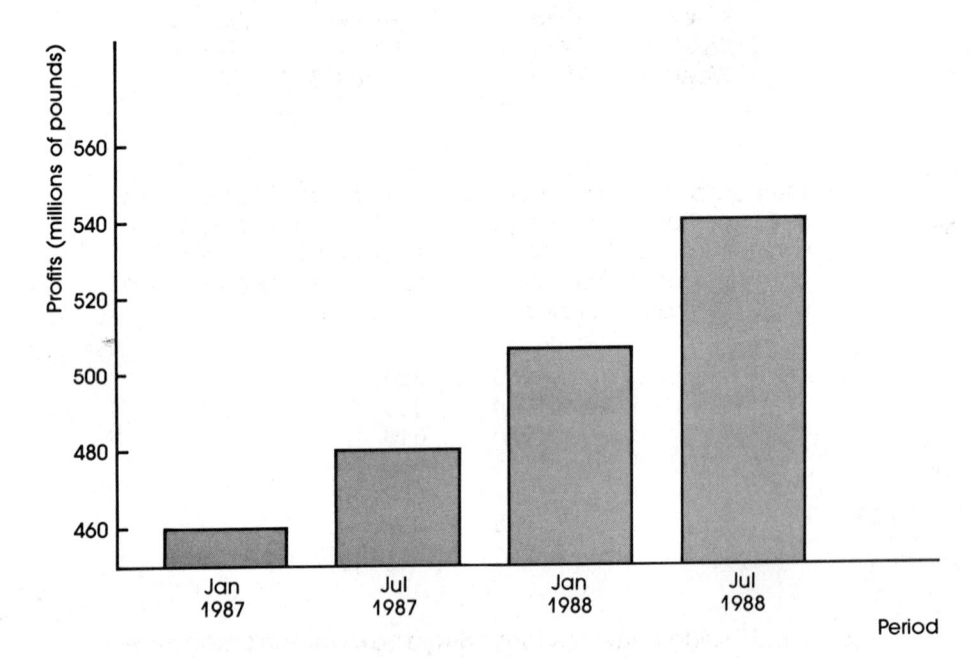

Figure 4.5

(a) Describe the effect that the bar chart's scale has on the look of the data.

(b) Draw another bar chart which has its scale starting at zero.

(c) How does this affect the look of the profits? Who might prefer the look of this diagram?

ACTIVITY 5

A bus company did a survey to see how people usually travelled to work. It asked 1000 people to name their usual means of transport and presented the results in a pictogram.

The company decided that the pictogram would be clearer if they used a different picture for each type of transport. To make the numbers 'easier', they also rounded them to the nearest 100. Here is the pictogram they produced.

Pictogram to show methods of travelling to work for 1000 people.

Car	🚙 🚙 🚙 🚙
Bus	🚌 🚌 🚌 🚌
Train	🚂
Other	👟

Figure 4.6

(a) How many people used the following types of transport?

  (i) Car
  (ii) Bus
  (iii) Train
  (iv) Other

(b) Are you sure these are the correct figures? What is missing from the pictogram?

(c) If you just looked at the pictogram quickly, which would you think was the most popular way of getting to work? What is it about the diagram that makes you think this?

(d) Which of the rules for pictograms does this one break? Do you think it was fair to round the figures off to the nearest 100? Here are the data that were actually collected.

>	Car 430
>	Bus 356
>	Train 146
>	Other 68

(e) How do you think that the numbers could have been rounded off more fairly?

(f) Draw another pictogram which obeys *all* the rules. Does it seem fairer?

Some diagrams can give a false impression by changing the *area* of the symbols, rather than just the height.

ACTIVITY 6

An advert was used to promote a new type of cereal. It was trying to show how much fibre was contained in each type of cereal. The people making the cereal wanted to show clearly that theirs had the most.

The actual figures in grams per 100 grams were

>	Cereal 1 4.3
>	Cereal 2 5.6
>	Cereal 3 7.9

(a) Has the company succeeded in making its cereal (number 3) look the best? Does the diagram make it look even better than it really is compared with the other two? How has this been done?

(b) How could this diagram be made fairer? What other ways could the data be shown so that it would give a clearer idea of the figures?

(c) Draw another diagram which is completely accurate and fair.

Here is the diagram used in the advert.

Three-dimensional bar chart to show comparison of fibre contents for three different cereals (grams per 100 grams).

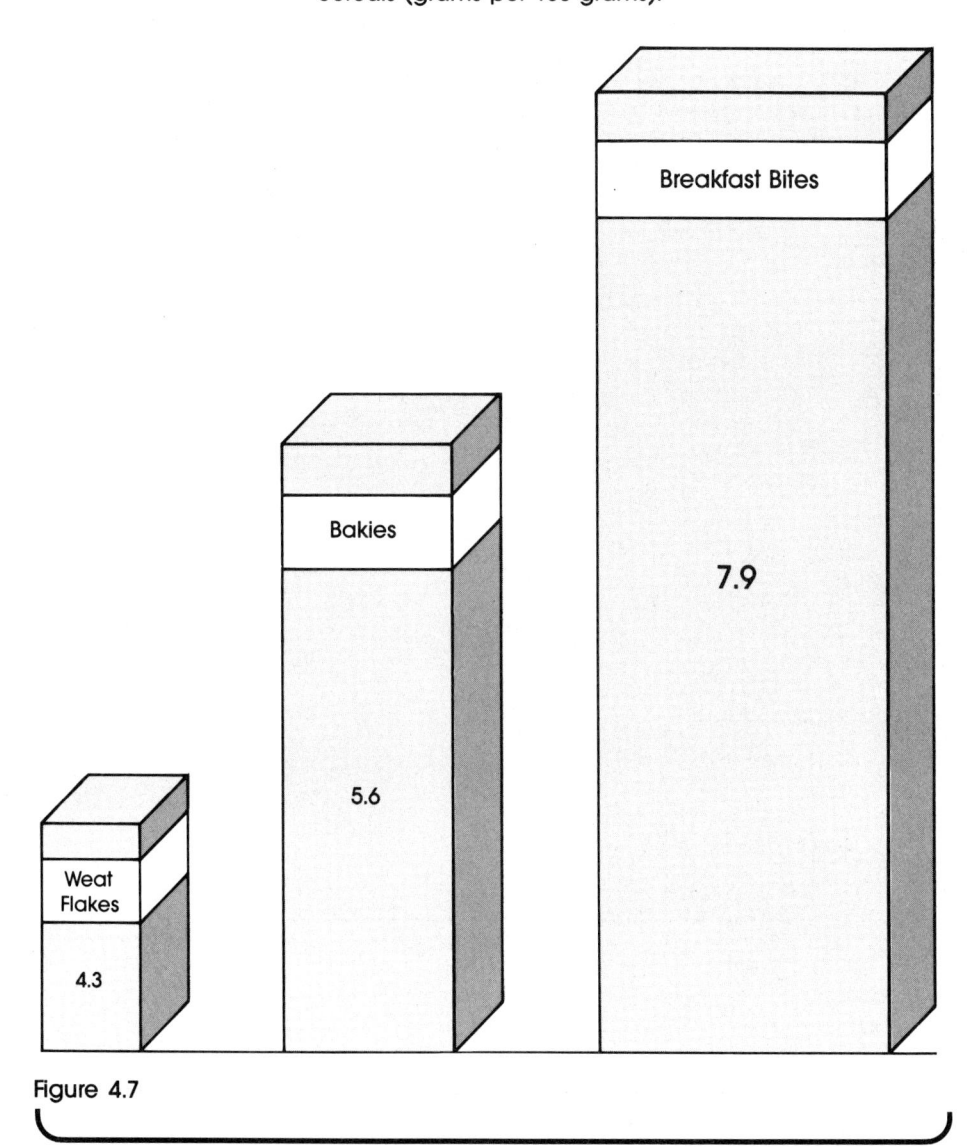

Breakfast Bites 7.9

Bakies 5.6

Weat Flakes 4.3

Figure 4.7

Other diagrams can give a false impression by making one part of the diagram look less attractive than another. This can be done by using bright and dull colours, strange shading which does not make the diagram pleasant to look at, or by changing the size of parts of it. You could try the colour and shading ideas when you do the project at the end of the chapter. Here is an example of the size trick.

ACTIVITY 7

A drugs company is launching a new version of aspirin called Aspain. It contains slightly more aspirin than normal tablets and the company wants to make the most of this fact in its advertising. Below is a copy of the diagram it used. Write down all the things which are wrong with this diagram. Using the fact that normal aspirin contains 300 mg of aspirin and Aspain contains 340 mg, produce a fair version of the diagram.

Bar chart to show aspirin content for two tablets.

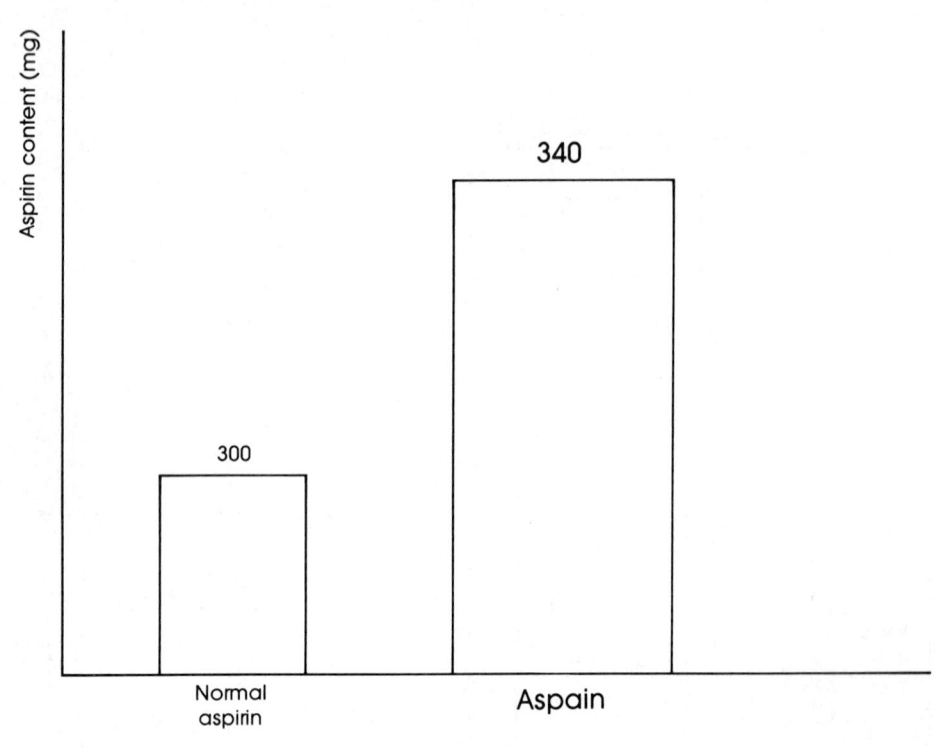

Figure 4.8

AVERAGES AND PERCENTAGES

We have already seen in Chapter 3 that we have to be very careful when using the word average, as it has several meanings. Some averages don't really mean very much! Some people actually use this fact to their advantage.

Discussion 1

The makers of a new hair spray put the following fact on their first advertisement.

8 out of 10 television stars use new Hold It

Discuss with your group or class what you think this statement really means and how you think they got the data. (It isn't actually a lie!)

Do *you* think that 80 per cent of *all* television stars will use the new hairspray?

What do you think that this statement *should* say if it were telling the *whole* truth?

Try to think of a current television advert which uses a statement similar to this one. Is it telling the *whole* truth? How do you think it should be changed?

ACTIVITY 8

A company advertising for new staff includes in its advert the statement

Our employees take home £180 per week on average

What *could* this statement mean? (Think of the three different ways of calculating the average. Is it the mean, median or mode they are talking about?)

If you were told that £180 was the *mean* amount earned and that the mode was £130, what could you say about the wages that the company pays?

In fact, 130 out of the 180 people earned £130 per week. What can you say about some of the other 50 people, remembering that the mean is £180?

ACTIVITY 9

A ferry company makes the following statement in its advertising.

No waiting! Average queueing time just 15 minutes!

If you have been on a ferry, does this sound about right?

To try to sort this out, we asked the ferry company how they had come by this figure. They said that the average figure was the mean of 1000 observations taken over a three-day period from Tuesday to Thursday in March.

What are your thoughts on this survey?

Think about the number of observations and the time period of the survey.

What do you think the ferry company should do in order to get a more realistic average waiting time?

Was the company telling lies in quoting the 15 minute figure?

ACTIVITY 10

A garage wants to show that it does its repairs and servicing quicker than any of its rivals. The owner wishes to quote average repair times in some advertising leaflets.

Describe the two ways in which these figures could be calculated, one to give a full picture and one to show that the garage is a little better than it really is!

What statistics could be collected, and when? Think how they could be used in each case.

Remember that you must not do anything which is dishonest or tell any lies, just 'play' with the statistics!

ACTIVITY 11

Read the following statements. We see statements like these in adverts from time to time.

(a) Now with 10% more cleaning power!

(b) 7 out of 10 people prefer it!

(c) Now up to 15% more in each packet!

Say what you think is misleading about each of these statements. Use these words to help you.

(a) Cleaning power?   (b) To what?   (c) Up to?

Look out for these sorts of statements in newspapers and television adverts. Write down any that you find. Is there any small print explaining what the advert actually means?

Here is a project for you to do.

ACTIVITY 12

Prepare some advertising for a new breakfast cereal. Some data is supplied but it is up to you to decide how to use them.

You will probably want to compare the cereal with other cereals and you will find plenty of information about them on the sides of packets. Have a look while you are eating your breakfast tomorrow and copy down or cut out the panel from the side of the packet.

Find a name for your new cereal. Here is some information about it.

Cost:
£1.10 per 400 g packet

Nutritional content (per 100 grams):

Energy	320 Calories	Vitamins:	
Protein	8 g	B6	1.6 mg
Fat	1.6 g	B2	1.7 mg
Carbohydrate	68 g	B1	0.8 mg
Fibre	9.8 g	D	2.3 µg
		B12	1.8 µg
		Iron	7.3 µg

Remember that if your cereal is better than all of the others in some way then you will want to make it look as dramatic as possible. If, on the other hand, the other cereals beat yours in some way then you will want to play this down and make them look as similar as possible.

Produce an advert for a magazine and a more detailed sheet to be sent to shop managers who will sell your product.

Remember, *no lies;* just use the statistics and the diagrams to your best advantage!

5 PERCENTAGES AND SCATTERGRAMS

PERCENTAGES

As well as using diagrams and averages, statistics are often presented in the form of percentages.

> **Discussion 1**
>
> Think about all the situations in which you have come across percentages.
>
> Note them down and then see how many different ideas there are in the class.

What does percentage mean? Well, literally, it means 'out of 100'. Any word beginning with 'cent' usually has something to do with 100. See how many you can think of. So if we say that 90% of homes have a television, it means that 90 out of every 100 homes have a television.

> **Discussion 2**
>
> Does this mean that if you visited 100 homes in your town, exactly 90 of them would have televisions?
>
> If not, what precisely does it mean?

Of course, the statistics which we need to collect do not always fall nicely into groups of 100! For this reason, we need to find a way of working out what percentage an amount is of a total. To do this, we can think of a percentage as a fraction of 100.

For example, we surveyed 600 people and asked them if they had a job (either full- or part-time). Of these 600, 444 said yes, the remainder said no.

To find out what *percentage* said yes, we need to find out the number *per hundred* which had a job. Since we have 6 hundreds, dividing the total by 6 will give us the correct figure. So:

$$444 \div 6 = 74$$

So 74 out of each hundred had a job, that is 74%.

Question 1

Here are the results of some other surveys. For each one, calculate the answers given as a percentage of the total. Use the method in the example above.

(a) 200 people were asked which was their favourite television channel; 126 said BBC 1.

(b) 300 people were surveyed; 153 were women.

(c) 500 people were surveyed; 265 were men.

(d) 1000 people were asked if they smoked; 830 said no, while 170 said yes.

This method works very well when the number of people surveyed is a multiple of 100, but of course very often it isn't. So what happens then? With a calculator, it isn't really a problem, because however 'nasty' the numbers, the calculator can cope!

A group of 140 pupils in a school were asked how many of them had school lunch. 112 of them said that they did.

To work this out as a percentage, we first work it out as a decimal fraction, that is

$$112 \div 140 = 0.8$$

This works out what *fraction* of the pupils have school lunch.

But this is a fraction of 1 rather than a fraction of 100. So to turn it into a percentage, we simply multiply by 100:

$$0.8 \times 100 = 80$$

So 80% of the children stayed for school lunch.

To do the calculation all at once, we would write:

$$112 \div 140 \times 100 = 80$$

This means that if you took 100 of these pupils at random, you would expect 80 of them to have lunch at school.

ACTIVITY 1

Do this survey in your own class. You will need to know how many people there are in the class and how many of them have school lunch.

If your percentage does not come out as a whole number, then round it off to the nearest one.

What percentage of the class does not stay for lunch?

What can you say about the total of the two percentages you have just calculated? Should this always happen?

To make sure that you have understood this method, try the following calculations.

ACTIVITY 2

Collect together the class's answers to the following questions. As you collect the figures, keep the answers of the boys and girls separately for the second part of the activity.

(a) Are you female or male?

(b) Have you any older sisters or brothers?

(c) Have you any younger sisters or brothers?

(d) Do you walk to school?

(e) Have you any dogs at home?

(f) Have you any elephants at home?

Present the answers to these questions for the class as a whole as percentages.

Now split the figures up into boys and girls. Calculate the percentages for the two sexes separately.

Careful! Are you dividing by the correct total each time?

It is just as easy to calculate percentages from very large survey samples, provided that you have a calculator to hand. Since it is not very easy for you to collect large amounts of data, some are provided below:

Results of GCSE exam survey
(A large number of students were asked how many subjects they had at each grade.)

Month exam taken	Grade								Total
	A	B	C	D	E	F	G	U	
June	6421	8367	9857	3425	4652	1697	984	784	36 187
November	564	894	962	1024	365	210	457	267	4743

ACTIVITY 3

Make a copy of the outline of the table above, including the column and row headings, but don't put in any of the numbers.

In each of the boxes fill in the percentage that the number represents of the total, instead of the number shown.

You will have to be very careful that you are using the correct total each time.

The first calculation is shown below. The answer is rounded to 1 decimal place, and you can do the same.

Month exam taken	A	B
June	6421 ÷ 36187 = 0.177 (Total for June exam) 0.177 × 100 = 17.7 17.7% gained grade A	

Using percentages in diagrams

Many of the types of diagram we have seen in earlier chapters can be adapted to use percentages and we shall look at some of them later.

PERCENTAGE STRIPS

There is one type of diagram, however, which is designed specially to use percentages. It is called a percentage strip.

It consists of a single strip representing the full 100%, which is then split up into sections according to the percentages which are required.

We surveyed 400 pupils in a school and asked them to name their favourite subject. The results are given below. We have not fiddled them (much!).

Maths	136	$136 \div 400 \times 100 =$	34% (to nearest 1%)
English	64	$64 \div 400 \times 100 =$	16%
PE	36	$36 \div 400 \times 100 =$	9%
German	45	$45 \div 400 \times 100 =$	11%
Science	85	$85 \div 400 \times 100 =$	21%
Others	34	$34 \div 400 \times 100 =$	9%
Total	400		100%

Having changed all the figures to a percentage of the total, we now divide up a strip into these percentages. This is much easier to do if the length of the strip is a multiple of 10 units long; for example 20 cm is quite a good length.

Since the whole 100% is represented by 20 cm, this means that 10% is 2 cm, 5% is 1 cm and so on.

Question 2

For each of the following percentages, say what length they would be represented by on a percentage strip which is 20 cm long.

(a) 50%   (d) 80%   (g) 1%
(b) 60%   (e) 25%   (h) 3%
(c) 30%   (f) 65%   (i) 9%

Here is a copy of the completed percentage strip for our subjects survey. It is 10 cm long. Check that the lengths are drawn correctly.

Percentage strip to show results of favourite subject survey.

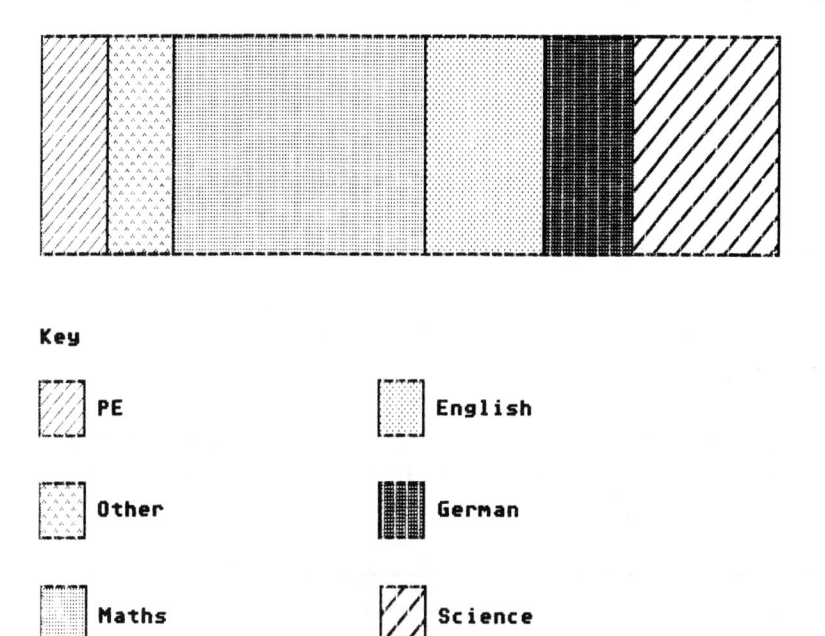

Key

- PE
- Other
- Maths
- English
- German
- Science

Figure 5.1

ACTIVITY 4

In the 1987 general election, the percentages of people voting for each party were as follows:

Conservative	43%
Labour	32%
SDP/Liberal	23%
Others	2%

Using these figures, draw a percentage strip to display the information.

ACTIVITY 5

Shortly after the general election, there was a by-election. The total number of people voting was 36 000, and they cast their votes for the following parties:

Labour	15 500
Conservative	13 200
SDP/Liberal	6450
Others	850

By first changing these data into percentage form, draw a percentage strip to display it.

Question 3

Compare the two percentage strips you have just drawn. Are they a good way of comparing two sets of data? Give reasons for your answer.

ACTIVITY 6

Take some of the figures from the table of exam survey results on page 69. Use your previous calculations to present the data in the form of a percentage strip. Check with your teacher which figures to use.

PERCENTAGE PIE CHARTS

As we said earlier, it is possible to use percentages in many types of statistical diagram. Pie charts are often used in this way. You will remember that the 360° in a pie chart are divided into sectors of differing sizes.

Question 4

If you split up the 360° of a circle into 100 equal divisions, so that each one represented 1%, how many degrees would be in each division?

> **Discussion 3**
>
> How would you deal with the fact that this would mean that a lot of your angles involved decimals, when it is really only possible to draw angles involving whole numbers?
>
> What if this led to your angles totalling 361° or 359°?

It is possible to get stencils to draw percentage pie charts which have percentages rather than angles marked on them. This makes life much easier! See whether your school has some.

ACTIVITY 7

Go back to the two sets of election data which you used earlier. Present the information as percentage pie charts. Do you think that this method makes comparison easier or more difficult?

ACTIVITY 8

Figure 5.2 shows three percentage pie charts. For each one, make a list of the categories shown and write next to each list your estimate of what percentage of the chart is represented by each.

ACTIVITY 9

Think of some of the other statistical diagrams which you have seen, for example bar charts, stem and leaf plots, etc. For each one say whether, and how, it could be adapted to use percentages.

Figure 5.2

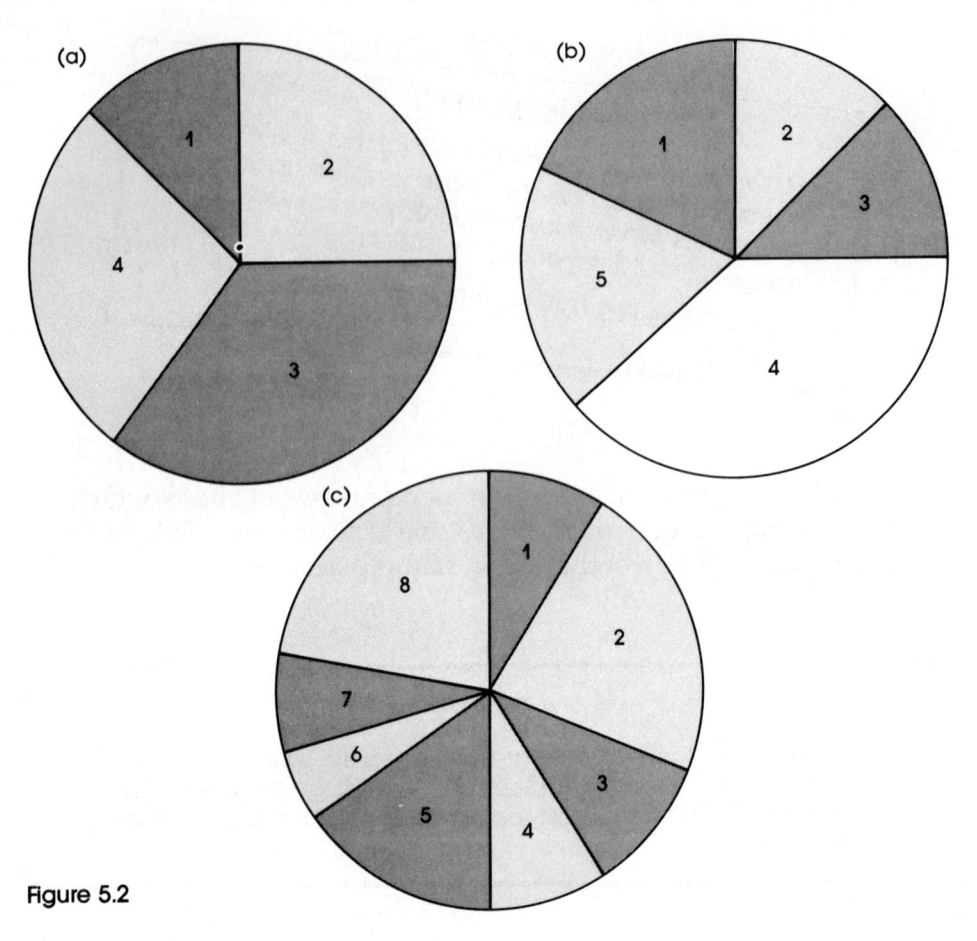

SCATTERGRAMS

Have you ever wondered whether two things are connected to each other? For example, is your height linked to your weight or to the speed at which you can run or to your shoe size?

You could do some tests to find out. But how would you present your results? All the types of diagram we have looked for so far have had only one set of information on them, not two. So we need a new type of diagram called a scattergram or scattergraph.

A scattergram has axes rather like a graph, with one set of data on each axis, and a cross or similar symbol to represent each point. Look at this example.

We surveyed the pupils in 2Z and asked them their height in cm and their weight in kg. We then plotted this information on a scattergram as follows. The weight was put on the horizontal axis and the height on the vertical axis. Neither of the scales starts at 0.

The first person in the survey weighed 55 kg and was 145 cm tall, so a cross was placed at the point (55, 145) on the graph. This is shown in Figure 5.3. The second person had a weight of 75 kg and a height of 167 cm so a second cross was placed at (75, 167).

By the time all the data had been put on the scattergram, it looked like the one in Figure 5.4.

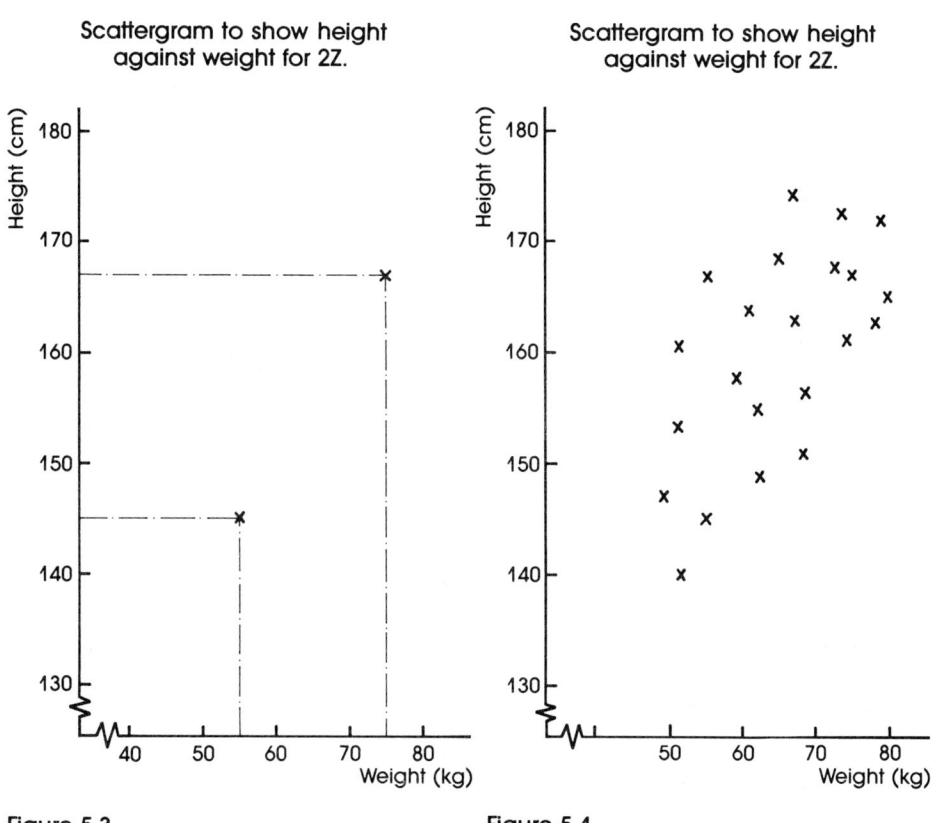

Figure 5.3

Figure 5.4

Discussion 4

Look carefully at the completed scattergram. Do you think it shows that the heights and weights of 2Z are connected?

Discuss your reasons with your group or class.

Do you think that all height-weight scattergrams would look like this?

So, to produce a scattergram, you simply plot each pair of data values as a coordinate on a graph. It is often not sensible to start the axes at 0, because, as in the case of height, there are often no very small values. Remember, though, to put on the symbol to show a non-continuous scale.

ACTIVITY 10

Collect some data for yourself for this activity. You could repeat our example of height and weight, but there are lots of other ideas.

For example, you could measure your height and your speed of running, the length of your arm or finger and your height, the results of tests in two different subjects, the distance you live away from school and the time you take to get there, or any of your own ideas.

Whatever your decide, collect the data, plot the scattergram and then try to decide if it shows a connection between the two sets of data or not.

So is there a connection?

The point of drawing a graph like this is to see whether two sets of data are connected, something which is difficult to see by just looking at the raw (original) data.

Figure 5.4 shows that in our height–weight survey there was a connection because, generally speaking, the taller people were also heavier. This made the points lie in a band which went from the bottom left to the top right of the diagram.

Question 5

Can you think of any other pairs of data which you think would be connected in this way?

Not all scattergrams display this sort of trend. Some show the data connected in other ways; others show that there is no connection at all between the two measurements.

ACTIVITY 11

Below are a number of scattergrams. They have no titles or labels on their axes, for a reason which will become obvious!

For each diagram, write down *how* you think the two variables are connected, giving reasons for your answer. Then, suggest what each set of data *could* be. Of course there will be no 'right' answer here, but there could be some wrong ones! If you have several suggestions, write them all down.

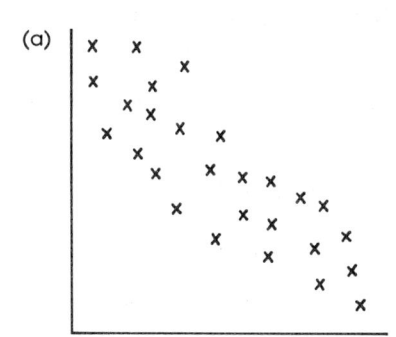

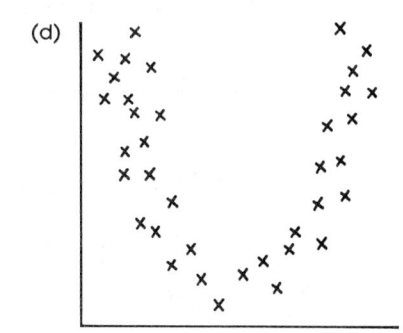

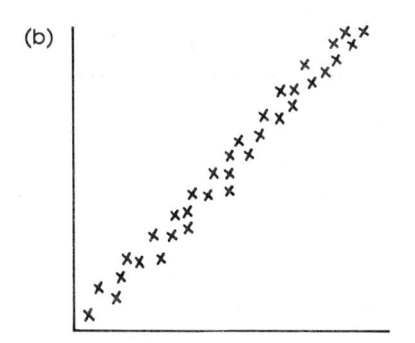

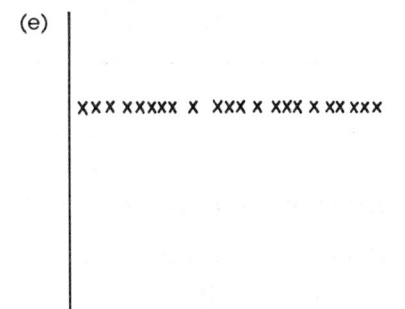

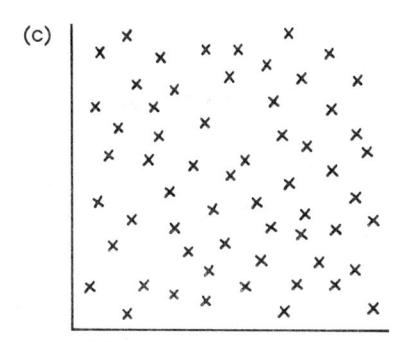

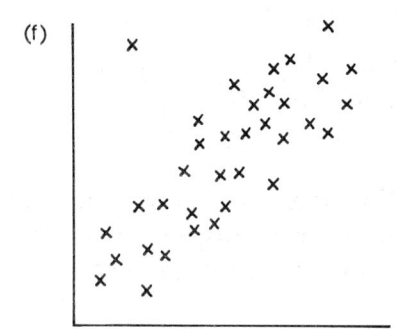

Figure 5.5

ACTIVITY 12

Now let's look at the problem the other way round. Below are some suggestions of pairs of data. Draw a sketch of the scattergram they would each produce. Obviously, these can't be accurate graphs, they are just to give a rough idea of how you think the two sets of data are connected.

(a) The numbers of goals scored by first division teams and their positions in the table at the end of the season.

(b) The lengths of runners' legs and the times they take to run 100 m.

(c) The costs of second-hand hatchback cars and their ages.

(d) People's heights and their scores in a physics test.

(e) The sizes of car engines and their top speeds.

(f) The costs of computers and the sizes of their memories.

(g) The costs of taxi journeys and their lengths (a taxi fare usually consists of a fixed charge plus a charge per mile of the journey).

Drawing lines on scattergrams

If a scattergram does show a connection between two sets of data, it is often helpful to draw a line on the graph so that other readings can be taken from it. This is sometimes called a **line of best fit**.

There are ways of calculating where this line should be; one way is to draw the line by eye. This means that you look to see where you think the line should go.

The basic idea is that the line should follow the general trend of the points you have plotted, and should have roughly equal numbers of points either side of it.

Figure 5.6, on the next page, shows how a line of best fit can be drawn on to a scattergram and how it can then be used for taking *estimated* readings of data values.

Scattergram to show marks gained in two tests.

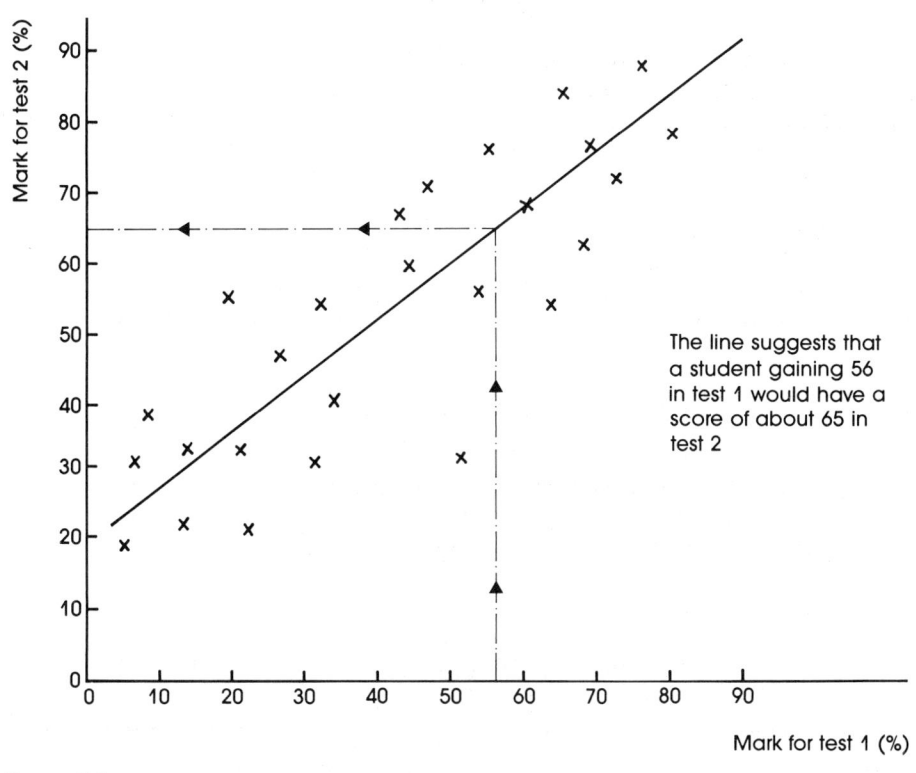

The line suggests that a student gaining 56 in test 1 would have a score of about 65 in test 2

Figure 5.6

ACTIVITY 13

Below are a set of data pairs. Use them to plot a scattergram, labelling the axes carefully. They are scores in French and German tests, both out of 70, with the German result given first.

(20, 25) (16, 20) (55, 35) (32, 35) (43, 40)
(40, 44) (49, 41) (64, 47) (12, 15) (36, 29)
(55, 50) (28, 23) (60, 56) (69, 61) (44, 32)

Draw a line of best fit on to the scattergram, and use it to find the following estimates.

(a) The French score of a pupil gaining 60 marks in German.

(b) The French score of a pupil gaining 25 marks in German.

(c) The German score of a pupil gaining 38 marks in French.

(d) The German score of a pupil gaining 53 marks in French.

ACTIVITY 14

Go back to the scattergram you drew for Activity 10. Draw a line of best fit on to each one and use it to estimate some values.

Of course, you have to be very careful when you look at scattergrams to be sure that there is *some* connection between the two sets of data. It is possible to make many sets of data *look* as if they are connected when in fact they have little or no correlation.

ACTIVITY 15

For this last activity in the chapter you are to do a bit of research. Try to find out the figures for the deaths from lung cancer over recent years. Also look for the numbers of people smoking and the numbers of people owning a car.

Plot the sets of data in various combinations on a scattergram and see if they show any correlation. Write a few sentences to explain what you see. Be careful!

6 FURTHER STATISTICAL METHODS

This chapter deals with some advanced statistical methods which you may need. These involve a lot of work with grouped data, as this is the way in which numerical data is often found.

CUMULATIVE FREQUENCY CURVES

Think about an examination board which sets, marks and grades thousands of exam papers each year. Once all the papers have been marked, it is up to the examiners to decide where to put the pass mark and the grade borderlines; that is to decide what percentage a candidate would need to get an A, B, C, etc.

To do this they may often want to ask themselves questions along the lines of

> How many people scored 40% or less?

or

> How many people scored 75% or more?

The statistical diagram which can be used to answer these questions is a **cumulative frequency curve.** Here is an example which will show how it works.

Having marked a maths test taken by 100 pupils, the teacher has recorded the marks obtained as follows.

Mark	Freq.	Mark	Freq.
1–10	3	51–60	24
11–20	6	61–70	14
21–30	11	71–80	6
31–40	13	81–90	3
41–50	18	91–100	2

This table shows that 3 pupils gained marks between 1 and 10, 6 scored between 11 and 20, and so on.

Question 1

How many people scored the following?

(a) 20 or less
(b) 40 or less
(c) 90 or less
(d) More than 70
(e) More than 60

Question 2

Why is it not possible to tell how many pupils scored 45 or less? Why might you want to know this?

Without looking at the original data (i.e. the pupils' individual scores) it is not possible to answer question 2 *exactly*, but it is possible to get a good estimate. To do this, you would first draw up a cumulative frequency table like the one below.

Mark	Cumulative freq.	
10 or less	3	
20 or less	9	(3 + 6)
30 or less	20	(3 + 6 + 11)
40 or less	33	(3 + 6 + 11 + 13)
50 or less	51	(3 + 6 + 11 + 13 + 18)
60 or less	75	(3 + 6 + 11 + 13 + 18 + 24)
70 or less	89	(3 + 6 + 11 + 13 + 18 + 24 + 14)
80 or less	95	(3 + 6 + 11 + 13 + 18 + 24 + 14 + 6)
90 or less	98	(3 + 6 + 11 + 13 + 18 + 24 + 14 + 6 + 3)
100 or less	100	(3 + 6 + 11 + 13 + 18 + 24 + 14 + 6 + 3 + 2)

As you can see, it is simply a running total, which is what cumulative frequency means. Notice the way in which the mark is described as '10 or less', etc. and the way in which the next range is included at each stage. From this table you can easily see that 89 people scored 70 or less, but we still can't answer question 2.

To do this we have to plot the curve. The horizontal axis is scaled with the mark and the vertical axis with the cumulative frequency, as shown in Figure 6.1. The points are then plotted on the diagram as shown in Figure 6.2. Notice how the crosses are plotted at the end of the original ranges, i.e. at 10, 20, 30, etc. These points are then joined to give a *smooth* cumulative frequency curve, as in Figure 6.3.

Question 3

Why do you think that the points are joined up with a curve, rather than straight lines?

It is now possible to answer question 2: how many people scored 45 or less? Find the score of 45 on the bottom axis, follow up to the curve and then across to the cumulative frequency axis. The number read off will be an approximate answer.

Question 4

Why is this not the exact answer? (If you find this difficult to answer think how much or how little you know about the 18 people who scored between 41 and 50.)

Question 5

By reading from the graph in Figure 6.3, find out how many people scored:

(a) 65 or less
(b) 87 or less
(c) 35 or less
(d) 48 or less.

Question 6

Remembering that there are 100 people in the survey altogether, work out how many people scored:

(a) more than 65
(b) more than 87
(c) more than 25
(d) more than 78.

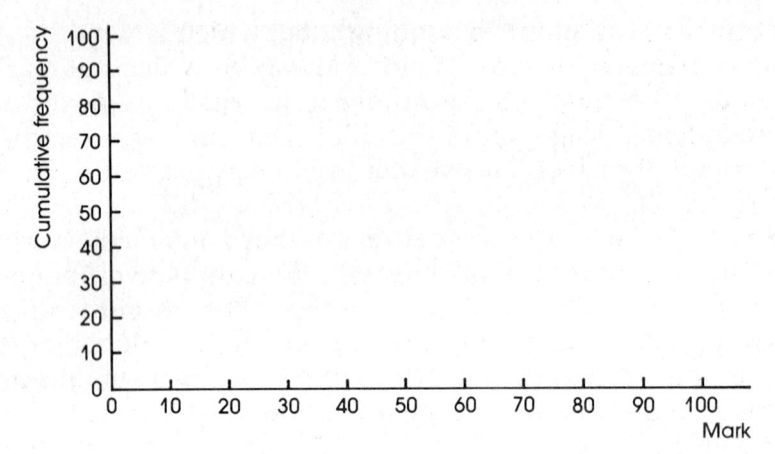

Figure 6.1

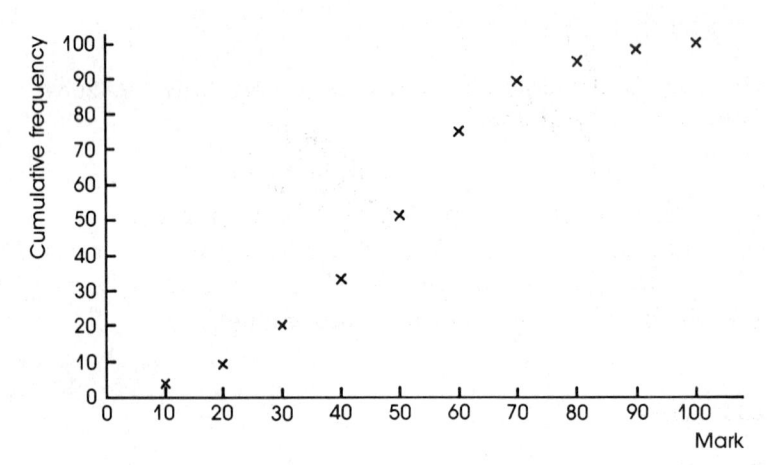

Figure 6.2

Cumulative frequency curve to show results of a maths test.

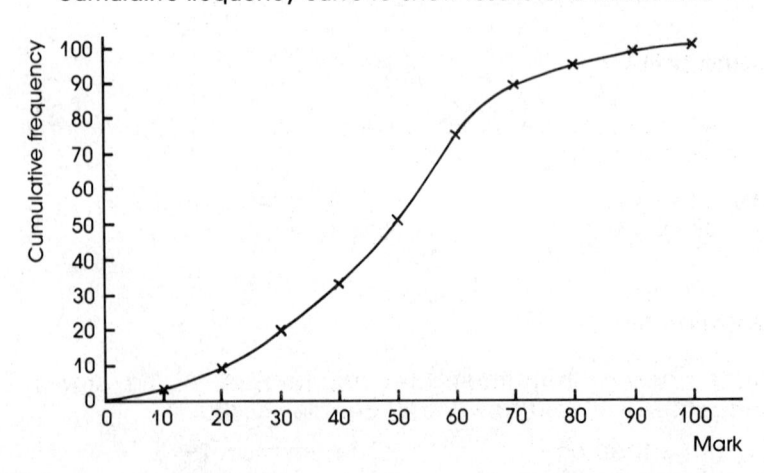

Figure 6.3

ACTIVITY 1

Here are some test results for 200 pupils in a school, presented in a similar way to those in the earlier example.

Mark	Freq.	Mark	Freq.
1-10	7	51- 60	42
11-20	11	61- 70	30
21-30	17	71- 80	19
31-40	22	81- 90	9
41-50	36	91-100	7

By first drawing up a cumulative frequency table, draw a cumulative frequency curve and then answer the following questions by reading values from your graph. Remember to make your graph a *smooth* curve, and give it a title.

(a) How many pupils scored 65 or less?

(b) How many pupils scored 85 or less?

(c) How many pupils scored more than 45?

(d) If the pass mark was 48, how many pupils passed the test?

You have now seen two cumulative frequency curves. If you compare them, you will see that their shapes are quite similar. This is no coincidence!

Question 7

By looking carefully at the data given, and in particular the *size* of the numbers, try to explain why the curve climbs steeply in the middle but is less steep at either end.

Discussion 1

Discuss your answer to question 7 with your group or class. Do you think this sort of stretched S-shape that you have seen will happen with all cumulative frequency curves? What would stop this shape appearing? What sort of data might it not appear with? If you plotted a graph of the frequency instead of the cumulative frequency, what do you think it would look like? Sketch it.

Taking averages and measures of spread from a cumulative frequency curve

There are several useful values which are easily obtained from a cumulative frequency curve. Probably the most common of these is the median. You will remember that this is the middle value, that is, it splits the data into two halves. It is found by taking the point half-way up the cumulative frequency axis, drawing across to the curve and then down to the horizontal axis, as shown in Figure 6.4. The median for this set of data is 49.5 marks.

Cumulative frequency curve to show results of a maths test.

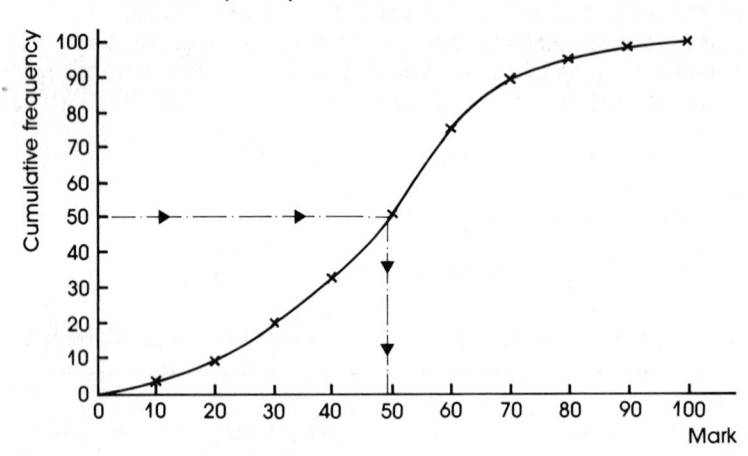

Figure 6.4

Of course, as you have seen when calculating the median, half-way between 1 and 100 is actually $50\frac{1}{2}$. Technically this means that you should draw across from 50.5 on the scale, but it makes very little difference, especially with fairly large samples of data, so 50 will do.

Because the cumulative frequency is a running total, it is particularly easy to find the middle value. You simply stop your running total when you are half-way through!

ACTIVITY 2

Go back to the graph you drew in Activity 1 and read off the median value in the way which was described. Try to be as accurate as you can.

Two other useful values that can be gained from a cumulative frequency curve are the **lower quartile** and the **upper quartile**. They are very similar to the median. They are the values that are one-quarter of the way and three-quarters of the way through the data. With the median they split the data into four equal parts. Quartiles are found from the graph in the same way as the median, as shown in Figure 6.5. The upper quartile is 60 marks and the lower quartile is 34 marks.

Cumulative frequency curve to show results of a maths test.

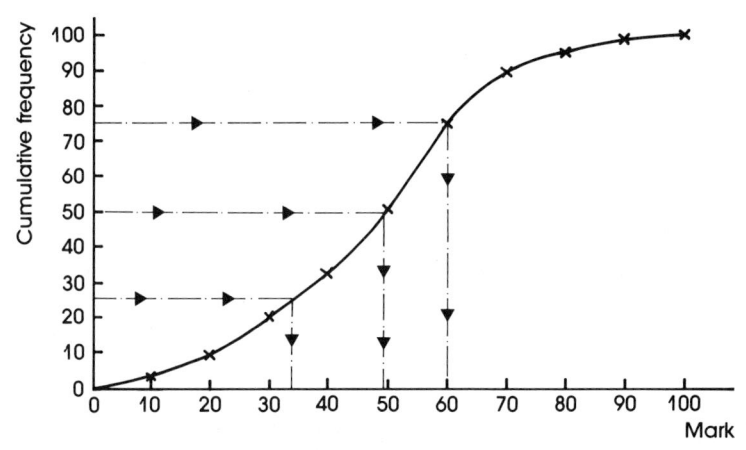

Figure 6.5

ACTIVITY 3

Go back to the graph from Activity 1 again and read off the values of the upper and lower quartiles.

A measure of how steeply the graph rises in the middle is given by the **interquartile range** (IQR). This sounds complicated, but it is simply the difference between the upper and lower quartiles. You just subtract the lower quartile from the upper quartile. In our example the IQR is 16.

ACTIVITY 4

Find the IQR for your graph from Activity 1.

Question 8

Why do you think the IQR measures the steepness of a graph? To help you decide look at the three curves in Figure 6.6 and put their IQRs in size order, starting with the *smallest*. Copy and complete the following sentence: A steep graph has a _____ IQR and a shallower graph has a _____ IQR.

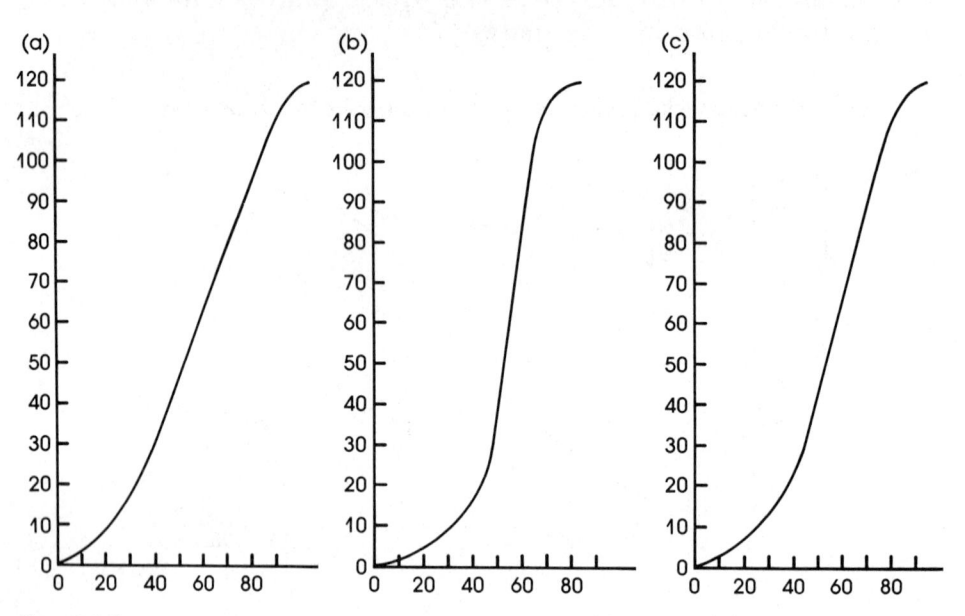

Figure 6.6

Activities 5, 6 and 7 show some data with which to practise these new techniques. If you would prefer to substitute some of your own data and then answer the same questions, but referring to *your* data, you can. (Ideas might include your own class's test results, heights, weights, or other measurements.)

Pause for thought!

Before you start to draw your cumulative frequency curves, here is a little problem for you to think about. Activity 5 looks at the lifetimes of some light bulbs, giving them in ranges of 200 hours. The first range is 201–400 hours.

Obviously, not all the bulbs lasted an exact number of hours, so these results must have been rounded to the nearest whole number. The first range could include bulbs that lasted from 200.5 up to, but not including, 400.5 hours, because this is the range of numbers which will round off to 201–400 to the nearest hour. Since the values for cumulative frequency curves are always plotted at the end of the range, this means that the first value should be plotted at 400.5, the second at 600.5, the third at 800.5 and so on.

ACTIVITY 5

We tested the lifetimes of a sample of 375 light bulbs. The results are recorded below.

Lifetime (hours)	Freq.
201– 400	56
401– 600	124
601– 800	101
801–1000	63
1001–1200	31

Draw up a cumulative frequency table, draw the curve and then read off the median, lower and upper quartiles. Calculate the interquartile range.

How many bulbs lasted more than 500 hours above average?

ACTIVITY 6

We surveyed 76 workers in a factory and asked them to tell us their take-home weekly pay. Here are the results, given to the nearest £.

Wage (£)	Freq.
81–100	6
101–120	14
121–140	21
141–160	19
161–180	11
181–200	5

Decide where each interval should start and finish, and then draw a cumulative frequency curve to display this data. What was the range of wages earned by the highest-paid quarter of the workers?

If the national average industrial weekly wage at the time was £136, how many workers at this factory do you estimate earned below the average?

ACTIVITY 7

As 85 people left a supermarket, we asked them how much they had spent. The results are recorded below, again rounded to the nearest £.

Amount spent (£)	Freq.
1–10	12
11–20	14
21–30	20
31–40	18
41–50	12
51–60	9

Decide where each interval should start and finish and draw a cumulative frequency curve for this data.

Find the median amount spent and the interquartile range.

Apart from the median and the quartiles, it is often useful to calculate other values. Another name for the median is the 50th percentile, because it is the value 50% of the way through the data. In the same way, the lower quartile could be called the 25th percentile and the upper quartile could be called the 75th percentile.

Other percentiles are found in exactly the same way. For example, the 10th percentile is the value 10% of the way through the data and the 90th percentile is the value 90% of the way through (10% from the top).

ACTIVITY 8

Using the graph you drew in Activity 7, calculate (a) the 90th, (b) the 10th, (c) the 40th and (d) the 70th percentiles.

HISTOGRAMS

Histograms are another way of presenting statistical data. At times, they appear to be very similar to bar charts, but they have several important differences. These are:

- They have a scale on the horizontal axis rather like a graph, rather than labels as on a bar chart.

- Frequency in each range is shown by the area of the bar, not the height of it.

- They allow unequal grouping of the data, e.g. 1–5, 6–15, 16–25, 26–45, etc.

- They are only suitable for purely numerical data, i.e. heights or weights. You could not use one for the results of a pets survey, as it would involve putting labels like dog, cat and mouse on the bottom scale rather than numbers.

Equal intervals

While you begin to understand how to construct histograms, we will stick to equal intervals with our grouped data. (These are often called **class intervals**.)

Look at the data below. You used it in Activity 5 earlier on, and it refers to the lifetimes of electric light bulbs.

Lifetime (hours)	Freq.
201– 400	56
401– 600	124
601– 800	101
801–1000	63
1001–1200	31

Recall that because these figures are given to the nearest hour, the intervals are really 200.5–400.5, 400.5–600.5, etc. These are the values at which your bars should start and finish.

To draw a histogram, first draw the horizontal axis, scaling it from 200 to 1200. Because the intervals are equal, the area of each bar will be the same as its height, if you think of it as having a width of 1 unit. So draw the bars so that their areas match the frequency, but don't write in a vertical scale. (You'll see why in a little while!)

You should now have a histogram similar to the one in Figure 6.7(a) on the next page.

(a) Histogram to show lifetimes of 400 electric light bulbs.

(b) Histogram to show lifetimes of 400 electric light bulbs.

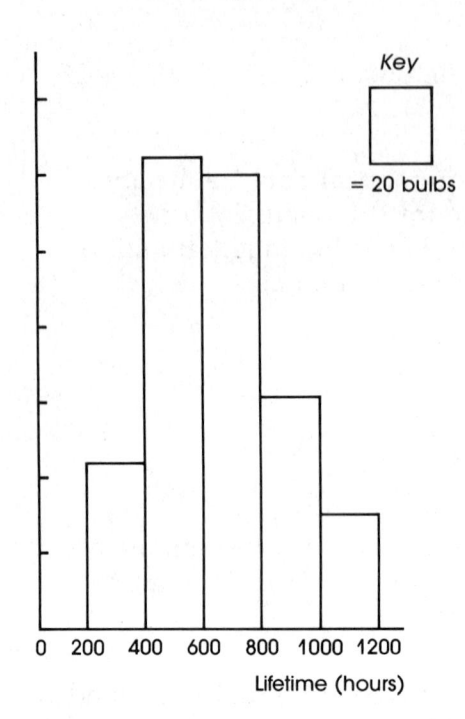

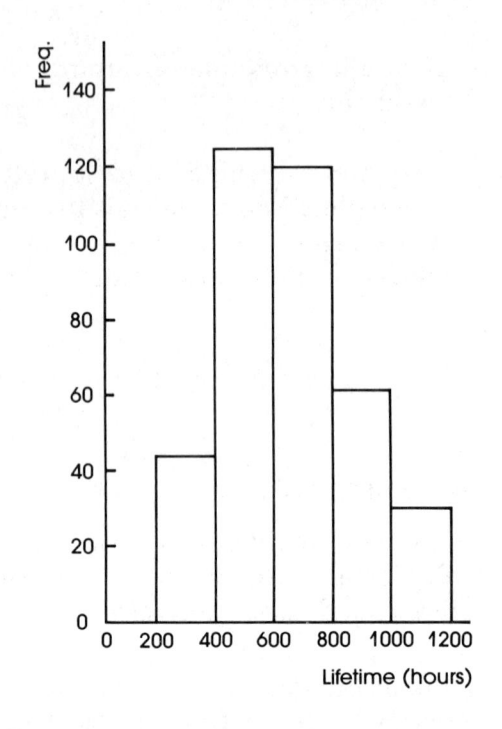

Key
□ = 20 bulbs

Figure 6.7

Notice that the scale is given by the small box showing what each unit of area represents.

If the data are classified into equal intervals as these are, then you can put on a vertical scale to show frequency (see Figure 6.7(b)). If you have unequal intervals, the next part of the chapter tells you what to do.

ACTIVITY 9

Go back to the data used for Activities 6 and 7, and use them to produce two histograms. Before you draw each one, think carefully about where the bars should start and finish. Remember to put on a scale for the area, and, as with any other diagram, it needs a title.

Unequal intervals

The first obvious question to ask about unequal intervals is why have them? What sort of data would be collected in unequal intervals?

> **Discussion 2**
>
> Try to think of some answers to our question. Think about our light bulb survey. Is it realistic, or might there be the odd bulb which would last much longer than the others? If you asked everyone in your school how far away they lived, would there be a few people who live quite a long way away? Would it be worth doing a whole new class interval just for them?

For our example, we'll look at some exam marks and grades.

Look at the following data. We saw them before at the beginning of the chapter.

Mark	Freq.	Mark	Freq.
1–10	3	51–60	24
11–20	6	61–70	14
21–30	11	71–80	6
31–40	13	81–90	3
41–50	18	91–100	2

The teacher setting this test decided to award grades to the pupils as well as giving them their scores. The grades were awarded as follows.

Mark	Grade
1–20	Fail
21–30	F
31–40	E
41–50	D
51–60	C
61–70	B
71–100	A

The teacher wants to see how many people fall into each category, and chooses a histogram with unequal class intervals to display the data. Although it may not be possible to score anything other than a whole number of marks, the easiest thing to do is still to draw the bars from 0.5–20.5, 20.5–30.5, 30.5–40.5, etc. This is a rule to stick to, whether or not non-whole number values are possible.

Notice that most of the intervals are of width 10 except two. The first interval has a width of 20 and the last one has a width of 30. We shall think of the width of 10 as being a width of 1 as far as calculating areas is concerned. So the 1–20 interval will have a width of 2 and the 71–100 interval will have a width of 3.

The calculations involved in working out the bar heights are shown in the table below and the completed histogram in Figure 6.8 on the next page.

Mark	Freq.	Width	Calculation	Height
1– 20	9	2	9 ÷ 2 = 4.5	4.5
21– 30	11	1	11 ÷ 1 = 11	11
31– 40	13	1	13 ÷ 1 = 13	13
41– 50	18	1	18 ÷ 1 = 18	18
51– 60	24	1	24 ÷ 1 = 24	24
61– 70	14	1	14 ÷ 1 = 14	14
71–100	11	3	11 ÷ 3 = 3.67	3.67

There are two ways of showing the scale: either put on an area scale as in Figure 6.8(a), or put a scale on the vertical axis. This should be marked 'Frequency per unit width' that is, it shows the frequency for the bars of width 1. To read off the frequency for bars of other widths, the frequency scale should be multiplied by the width of the bar.

This is quite sensible because what you are doing is finding the area of the bar, and we have already said that frequency on a histogram is shown by the area of the bars. This is shown in Figure 6.8 (b).

You now have a completed histogram.

(a) Histogram to show marks gained by pupils in school test.

(b) Histogram to show marks gained by pupils in school test.

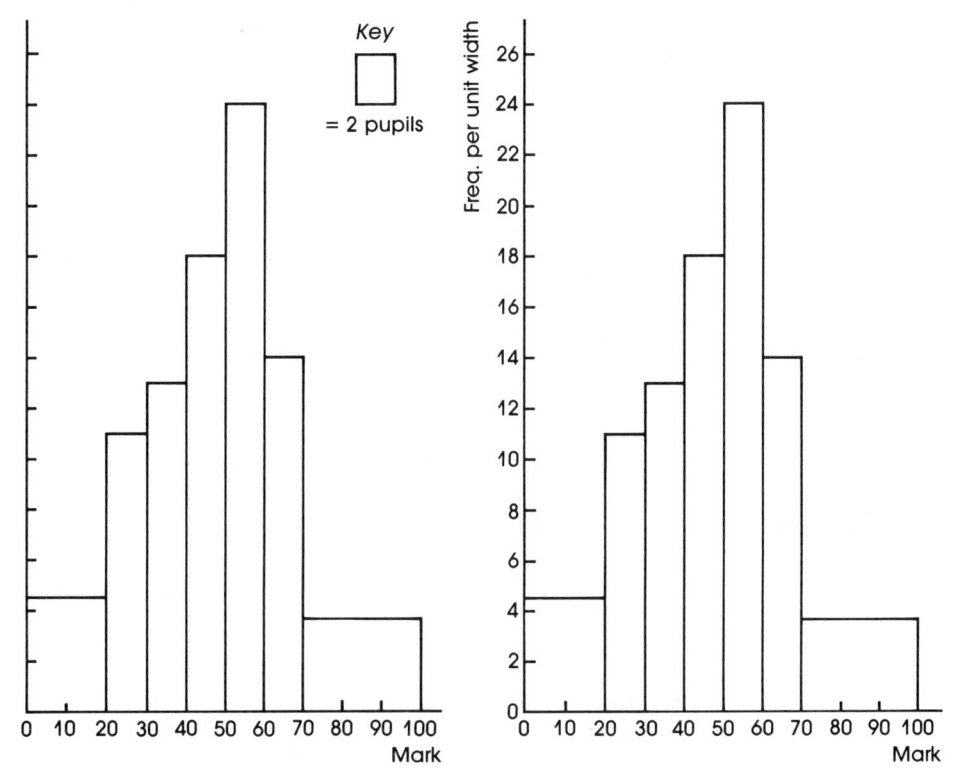

Figure 6.8

ACTIVITY 10

We asked 100 children to say how much money they had in their bank accounts. Here are the results given to the nearest £.

Amount (£)	Freq.
1– 10	5
11– 20	8
21– 30	15
31– 40	23
41– 50	16
51– 70	8
71– 90	9
91–130	16

Taking an interval of £10 as a width of 1 unit, draw a histogram to show this information. Scale your diagram using the method you prefer. Remember that these figures are to the nearest £.

ACTIVITY 11

We surveyed the number of children in each type of school in a large area of England. Below are the results.

Type of school	Age range	Freq. (thousands)
Nursery	2– 4	320
Primary	5–10	6235
Secondary	11–16	7254
Sixth form	17–19	241

First, decide where each bar is going to start and end. Ages aren't the same as money. When do you stop describing someone as 4 years old? Not when they pass four-and-a-half!

Draw a histogram to display this information, using sensible bar widths.

ACTIVITY 12

The heights of 200 people were measured to the nearest centimetre and the results are recorded below.

Height (m)	Freq.
1.35–1.54	26
1.55–1.64	35
1.65–1.74	42
1.75–1.84	67
1.85–1.99	30

Display these data using a histogram.

AVERAGES FROM GROUPED DATA

Once data has been put into groups you 'lose' some of the information. You can no longer see the original measurements or results, only the number of items which lie in a particular range.

This makes the calculation of averages rather more difficult. It means that it is often only possible to get an estimate of an average rather than its exact value, although this is often good enough.

Mode

It is not possible to find the mode from grouped data, and estimating it is quite involved. However, it is very easy to say which is the **modal class**. This is simply the group or class which contains the mode, i.e. the highest bar on the histogram.

Mean

You can't calculate the mean exactly because you do not know what the original data looked like, but you can get a good estimate. To calculate the mean, assume that all the items in a particular class have the middle value of this class. Here are the heights data you used in Activity 12.

Height (m)	Freq.
1.35–1.54	26
1.55–1.64	35
1.65–1.74	42
1.75–1.84	67
1.85–1.99	30

The mid-point of the first group is 1.445 m. (This value is obtained by averaging the start and end values of the interval.) We assume that all 26 people in this group have this 'average' height. Similarly we assume that the next 35 people all have a height of 1.595 m, and so on. The mean is then calculated in the usual way:

$$\text{Total} = (26 \times 1.445) + (35 \times 1.595) + (42 \times 1.695) + (67 \times 1.795) + (30 \times 1.92)$$

$$= 342.45$$

$$\text{Mean} = 342.45 \div 200$$

$$= 1.71 \text{ m} \quad \text{(to 2 d.p.)}$$

Discussion 3

Think why this is not the exact mean. How good an estimate do you think it is? What assumptions have been made? In what circumstances would this be a bad estimate?

Median

It is possible to get an estimate of the median by using a table of data, but it is rather complicated. It is easier to use the method of drawing a cumulative frequency curve as you saw earlier in the chapter.

ACTIVITY 13

Using the data in Activities 10 and 12, calculate estimates for the mean of the data and state the modal class.

---

7 STATISTICAL PROJECTS

This chapter discusses some of the things you will have to think about if you are going to do your own statistical project. You may be doing a piece of GCSE coursework, or simply a piece of work in class. Whichever it is, these are the stages you should go through in planning your project.

- Think of a question you would like an answer to.
- Decide how to answer it.
  What statistics are required?
  How are you going to collect them?
- Collect the data.
- Decide how you are going to present the data.
  Diagrams?
  Calculations?
- Analyse your results.
- Present your conclusions.

Of course, it may not always go as smoothly as this! You may get to the point where you are ready to analyse your results and find that you have not got sufficient data, so you might have to go back a few stages and do some more preparation.

THINKING OF A QUESTION

The first thing to do is to think of a question you would like an answer to. Try not to think of statistics you could collect (e.g.

house prices) and then wonder what you could do with them. Instead, think of a question like:

> Are houses prices on the north side of town higher than on the south side, and if so why?

and then plan *how* to answer the question.

Your question should be quite specific and not too 'woolly', so that you can plan exactly what you are going to do.

DECIDING WHAT DATA TO COLLECT

Once you have decided on your question, you must then decide what data you will need and how you are going to get it.

If you need information from people you may well have to design a questionnaire. There may be measurements to take, observations to record or it may be that someone else has already collected the data for you and you will have to go and find it in a library, in reference books or government publications.

It may not even be obvious what data to collect! For example, if your question was 'Are newspapers politically biased?', you may have a good idea of the answer yourself, but it might be quite difficult to decide how to measure it statistically.

Discussion 1

Think about the question described above and decide upon some methods of measuring any bias.

QUESTIONNAIRES

Designing a suitable questionnaire is not as easy as you might think. If you do not get the questions right you may well find that, having asked people to answer them, you can't really find the answers which you wanted or you can't find a way of presenting your results.

ACTIVITY 1

Here are some sample questions from surveys. For each one, say how good a question you think it is and how you would present the results. If you think it is a bad question, try to reword it so it would get better results.

(a) How do you vote?

(b) Do you think the buses are good around here?

(c) Are books too expensive?

(d) What do you think of the school meals?

(e) Do you think home computers are a waste of money?

(f) If there was a general election tomorrow, for which party would you vote?

(g) How do you usually travel to school?
Bus
Car
Walk
Cycle
Other

(h) On a scale of 1 to 5, how satisfied would you say that you were with your local radio services?

SAMPLING

If you are going to do surveys or give out questionnaires, how are you going to decide who to give the questionnaire to?

Discussion 2

If you went into your town centre on an average weekday and stopped the first 30 people you saw, what type of people would they be likely to be? Would this bias your survey? In what ways? How could you avoid this?

> **Discussion 3**
>
> If you were doing a survey within your school, how would you choose the people you were going to ask to make sure that you got an unbiased sample of people?

BIAS

Apart from getting an unbiased sample of people, you must also make sure that your questions are unbiased. That is, you must make sure that they do not make people more likely to give one answer than another.

> **Discussion 4**
>
> Look at these two pairs of questions.
> (a) Do you like dull colours like brown and dark blue?
> Do you like nice warm colours like brown and dark blue?
> (b) Do you think it is right to take away people's right to smoke in public places?
> Do you think that anti-social and unhealthy habit of smoking should be banned in public places?
>
> What difference do you think there would be if we asked 100 people each of these questions?
> You could test out this way of biasing questions by designing two separate questionnaires which ask the same questions, but phrased in different ways. You will have to remember, of course, that there may be other things which affect people's answers.

COLLECTING THE DATA

Once you have planned what you are going to do, you must then collect the data. Make sure that you do this in an organised way!

Remember, for example, the five-bar tally method for recording frequency and make sure that your tables of results, even the rough versions, are neatly drawn.

You may also have to decide upon a level of accuracy. For example, if you were going to measure 30 people's heights would you do it to the nearest centimetre or to the nearest millimetre? Also, make sure that you tell people what units you would like them to use when answering your questions.

PRESENTING YOUR RESULTS

The first six chapters of this book give details of lots of ways of presenting statistical information. Some methods are particularly good in some circumstances, and it is important that you make the right choices.

ACTIVITY 2

Look at each of the following sets of data and decide the best ways of presenting them. There will be more than one way for many of them. Remember all the different types of diagrams and calculations and try to use a variety of them.

(a) 100 answers to a simple yes/no question.

(b) Comparisons of girls' and boys' answers to a question.

(c) An analysis of house prices in an area of your town.

(d) A 'favourite subjects' survey.

(e) A comparison of three different sets of test results taken at different times of the year.

(f) A comparison of forecast and actual temperatures during a two-week period.

(g) A comparison of attendances at different football clubs on a given Saturday in the season.

(h) An analysis of use of space in a newspaper.

Discuss your answers in small groups.

ANALYSING RESULTS AND PRESENTING CONCLUSIONS

It is important to know the limitations of your work. The sample of people or things from which you have collected your statistics or made your observations will probably be quite small. For this reason you must not make sweeping generalisations. That is, if you have interviewed 30 people in your town, you can't say that they were representative of the whole country, or even of the whole town for that matter.

You might say that from your results it would appear that . . . , or that your results suggest that . . .

Present all your diagrams carefully and make sure they all have titles and keys or scales. If you quote averages, say which they are and if you use percentages, make sure that it is obvious to the reader what they are percentages of.

Look for patterns in your data and diagrams that will help explain your results and try to suggest reasons why these patterns are present.

ACTIVITY 3
Look at the data displayed in the three diagrams of Figure 7.1 on the next page. Describe carefully the patterns which they show, and try to give reasons for them. Discuss your answers.

IDEAS FOR PROJECTS

The final section of this chapter gives some ideas for your project work. These are only broad outlines and you must turn them into real problems by *thinking of a question to which you would like to know the answer!*

Many of the ideas will need adapting to your school or your town, but they should give you some things to think about.

Analysis of books

Many projects can be based on analysing the way books are written. For example, you could take different books written for children of different ages and ask yourself 'Are the words used easy enough for the average reader of that age?' You could look at children's books to see if they use sexist ideas, or whether modern books are less liable to do this than older ones.

(a) Graph to show temperature during a 24-hour period in May.

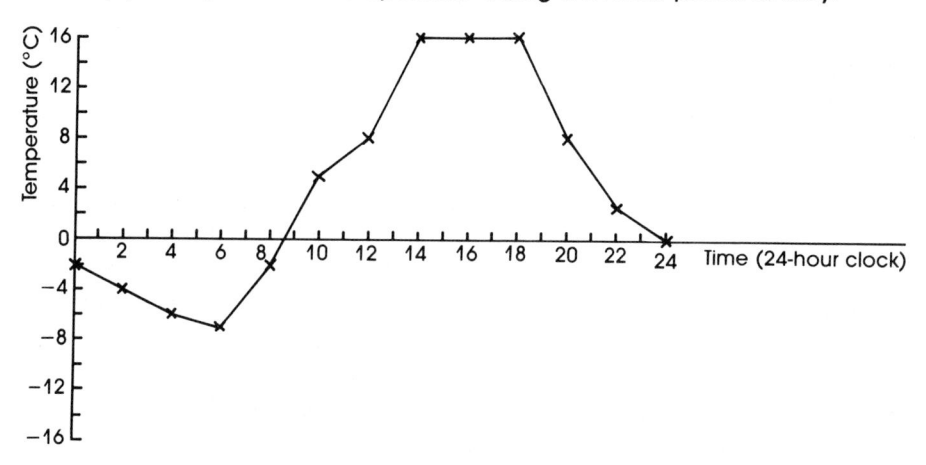

(b) Bar chart to show totals gained on two dice thrown many times.

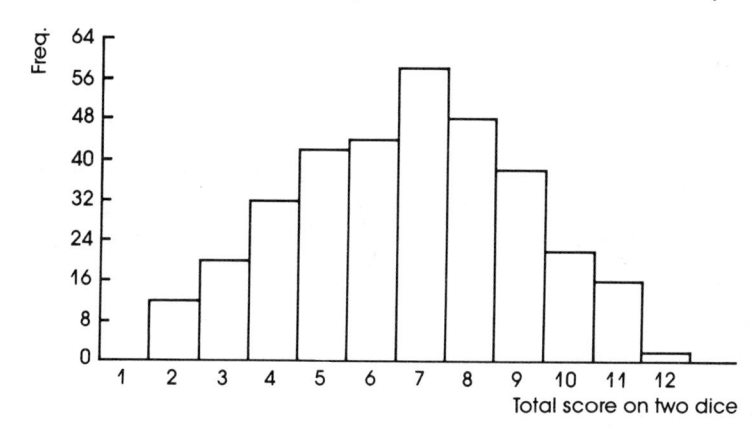

(c) Pie chart to show results of survey of 100 children's favourite colours.

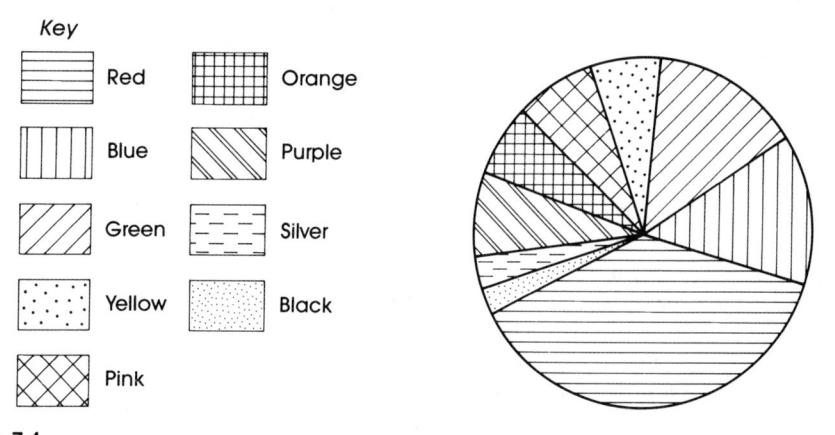

Figure 7.1

Can you tell who wrote a book by analysing the lengths of words or sentences? You may be able to find some results of analysis that has been done on the works of Shakespeare. There has been argument in the past about whether he really wrote all of his work. Similar arguments have begun about more modern authors.

In a similar way you could analyse the use of different letters in different languages. Instruction books are good for this because they often have exactly the same piece of text written in four or five different languages. For example, you could look at which vowels are the most popular in each of the languages. Once you've done your analysis, you could design little puzzles for others to solve. Give them each an analysis of a passage of text and ask them to compare it with your results. They could then try to work out which language it was written in. You may be able to use a text analysis program on a computer which automatically counts the word lengths or letter usage as you type in the text. Ask whether your school has a program like this.

School meals

Are the pupils in your school satisfied with the school meals? Are they happy with the canteen arrangements? You could carry out some observations to see what improvements could be made or design a questionnaire to get pupils' views.

Advertising and television

Chapter 4 showed how statistics can be made to show things in a dramatic way to help in advertising. You could ask the question 'Is all advertising fair?' and analyse how statistics are used in advertising. On a similar theme, you could look at the use of statistics on television, especially in current affairs and news programmes. Is the truth ever exaggerated to make a point?

Traffic and roads

Does your town need a new pelican crossing? Does it need a by-pass? Do you need a crossing outside your school? What do people in your town think? Is there too much heavy traffic going through the centre of your town or near your school?

There is a lot of scope here for questionnaires, traffic surveys and for finding out how the professionals do it. Has your local council organised any traffic surveys recently? If so, what were the results?

Your local council may have information about recent road traffic accidents which you could analyse. When do most accidents happen, who do they involve and how could they be prevented? Your local police might have more information.

Computer databases

One of the main advantages of computers is that they can handle lots of information very quickly. A database is a computer system which allows you to store lots of information and then search for a particular fact. Lots of census data are stored on computers and many questions can be answered by interrogating the computers. For example, how has employment changed over the years, or how have the sizes of families altered? You may be able to get hold of census information from as far back as 1851 and compare it with that from the present day. Your school might already have some, or you could ask at your local town hall.

You might like to use a data handling program to record the results of your own questionnaire and to produce results. Some programs can display pie charts, histograms and other diagrams which you may then be able to print out to use in your project.

You may find that information has been coded on the computer to save memory space, and you might have to code your own information.

General surveys and questionnaires

You can construct a questionnaire about almost anything. You must be careful not to ask people about things which are private or personal. For example, many people will not want to answer questions about their incomes or their family lives, so *be careful!* The last thing you want to do is offend the people from whom you are trying to get information.

Here are some ideas for topics.

- Luxury goods: which items do people think are the most important out of televisions, videos, washing machines, tumble dryers, stereos, microwaves, etc. and how much would they be willing to pay for them? Which have they already got?
- Pets: what pets do people have? How do their jobs or family sizes affect the type of pet which they have? How do people feel about having dog licences or dog wardens?
- Television: are people satisfied with the television service? How do they think it could be improved? What style of programme do they watch most often? What should there be more and less of? What do they think about the licence fee?

- Banks: what do people think about the services which their banks offer them? Which banks do they use? Why? Would they swap banks if their branch did not have a cash machine and another bank installed one in their area? The same sort of investigation could apply to other services.

Sports

Are attendance figures at football matches falling, rising or steady? Why have some people stopped going to watch matches? What do these people do instead? Has television coverage affected attendances? Are entrance fees sensibly priced? What would make more people go to football matches? Are there differences between the attendance figures in different areas of the country?

There are plenty of ideas for sports fans, and you don't have to stick to football. Attendance figures are published in some of the Sunday papers, or you will find them in football yearbooks if you want to go back to previous years.

House prices

It is sometimes difficult to collect enough data for this type of project, but you shouldn't find too many problems if you live in quite a big town or city. You can get data from either the local estate agents or the local papers. Do prices for similar types of houses vary in different parts of your town or city? If so, how? Could you get information from other parts of the country and compare prices? (Perhaps you have friends or relatives in different parts of the country who could send you information.)

You could also look at different facilities and see what appears to increase the price. Does central heating or a fitted kitchen increase the price?

Personal skills

There are plenty of skills you can test, if people will take part! You could investigate estimation skills, such as angles, lengths, volumes, areas, number of peas in a jar. You can also test people's reaction times, perhaps using a computer program which asks them to press a particular key on the keyboard. Are girls quicker than boys? Are left-handed people quicker than right-handed ones?

You could also test the effect of one activity on another. Does physical activity (e.g. running) affect reaction times? Does lack of food affect concentration? (Please don't starve anybody!)

8 QUESTIONS FOR EXTRA PRACTICE AND REVISION

This chapter consists of questions which can be used for extra practice and revision. They are in seven sections. The first six sections correspond to Chapters 1 to 6; the final section consists of questions of GCSE mathematics standard.

CHAPTER 1

Question 1

A survey asked people to name the city they would most like to visit from a list of four. The results are shown in the bar chart below.

Bar chart to show results of favourite city survey.

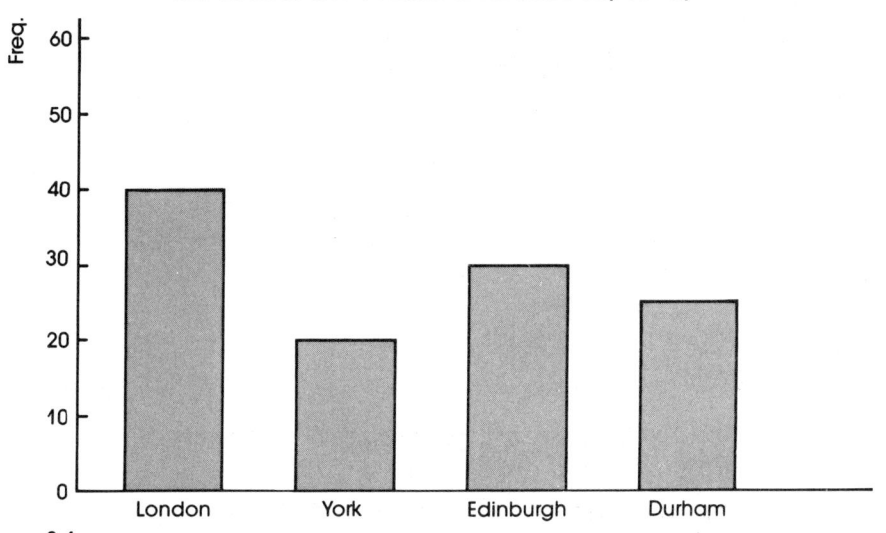

Figure 8.1

(a) Which was the most popular city?

(b) Which was the least popular?

(c) How many people chose York?

(d) How many people took part in the survey altogether?

Question 2

The money given to a school for one year was divided up amongst the departments as shown in this pie chart.

Pie chart to show division of one year's money in a school.

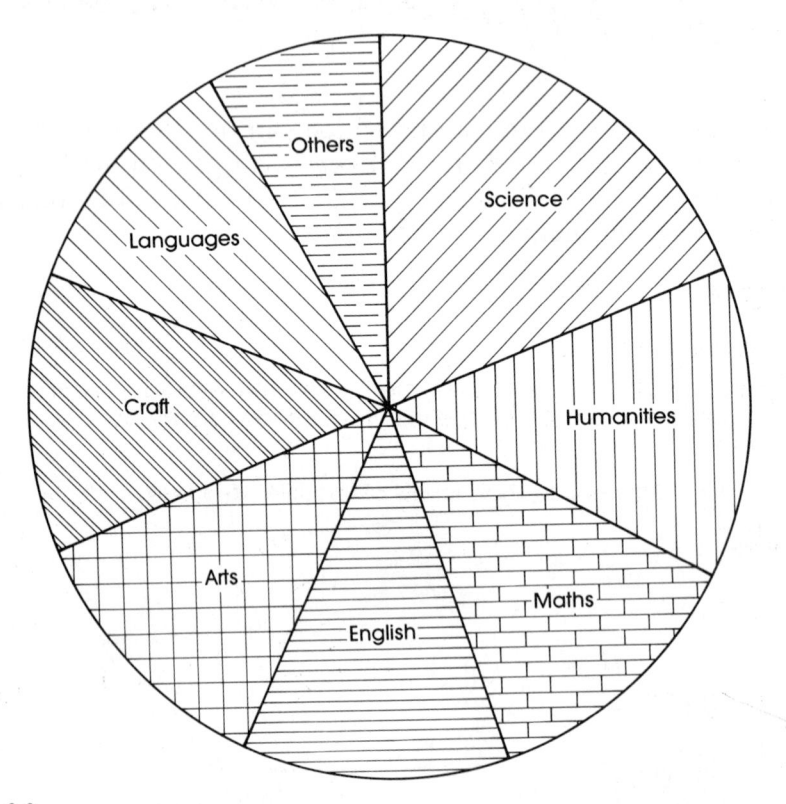

Figure 8.2

(a) Which department got the most money?

(b) Name two departments which got the same amount of money.

(c) About what fraction of the money did the English department get?

Question 3

The weekly sales of singles in a record shop are displayed on the following graph.

Line graph to show weekly sales of singles in a record shop over a seven week period.

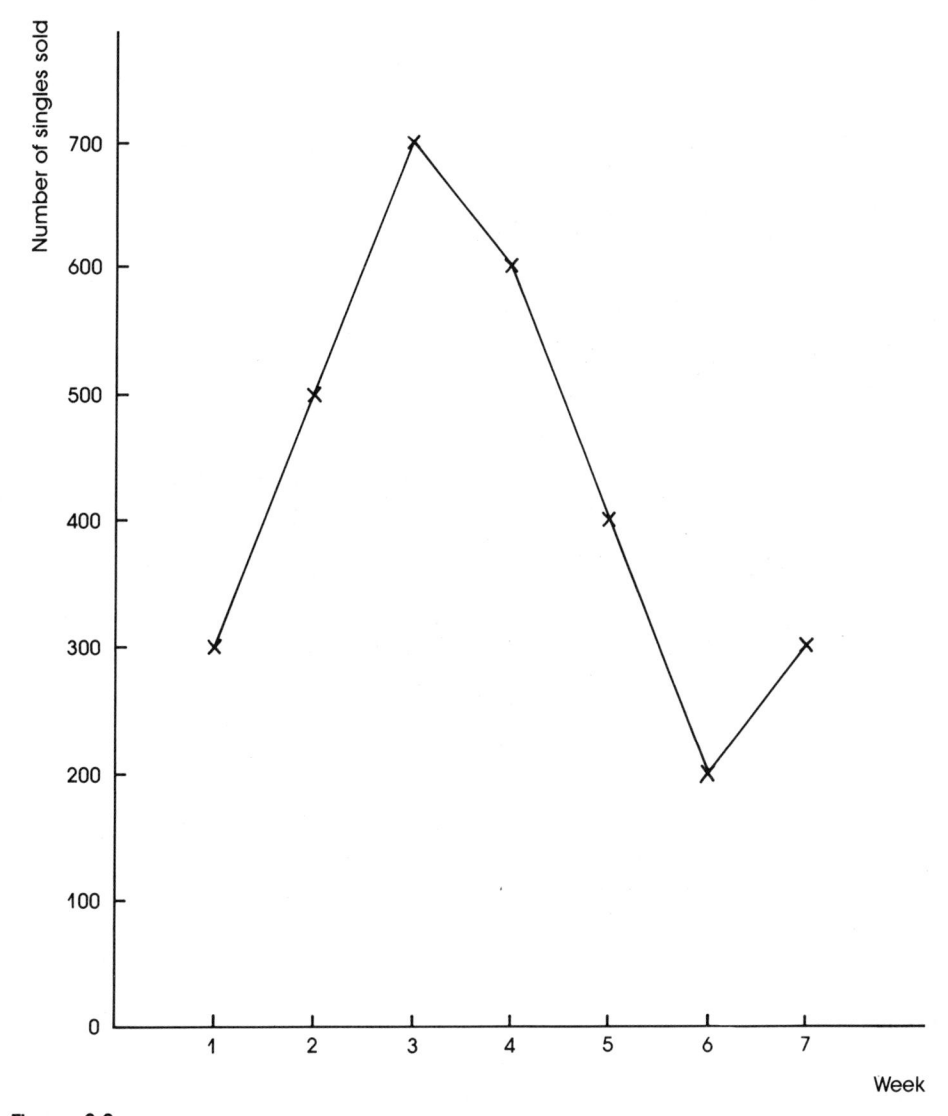

Figure 8.3

(a) Write down the number of singles sold in each of the seven weeks.

(b) Describe in your own words the pattern of sales during these seven weeks.

Question 4

A group of second-year pupils was given the chance to take one craft subject from a list of five. Their choices are shown below.

Pictogram to show second-year pupils' choices of craft subjects.

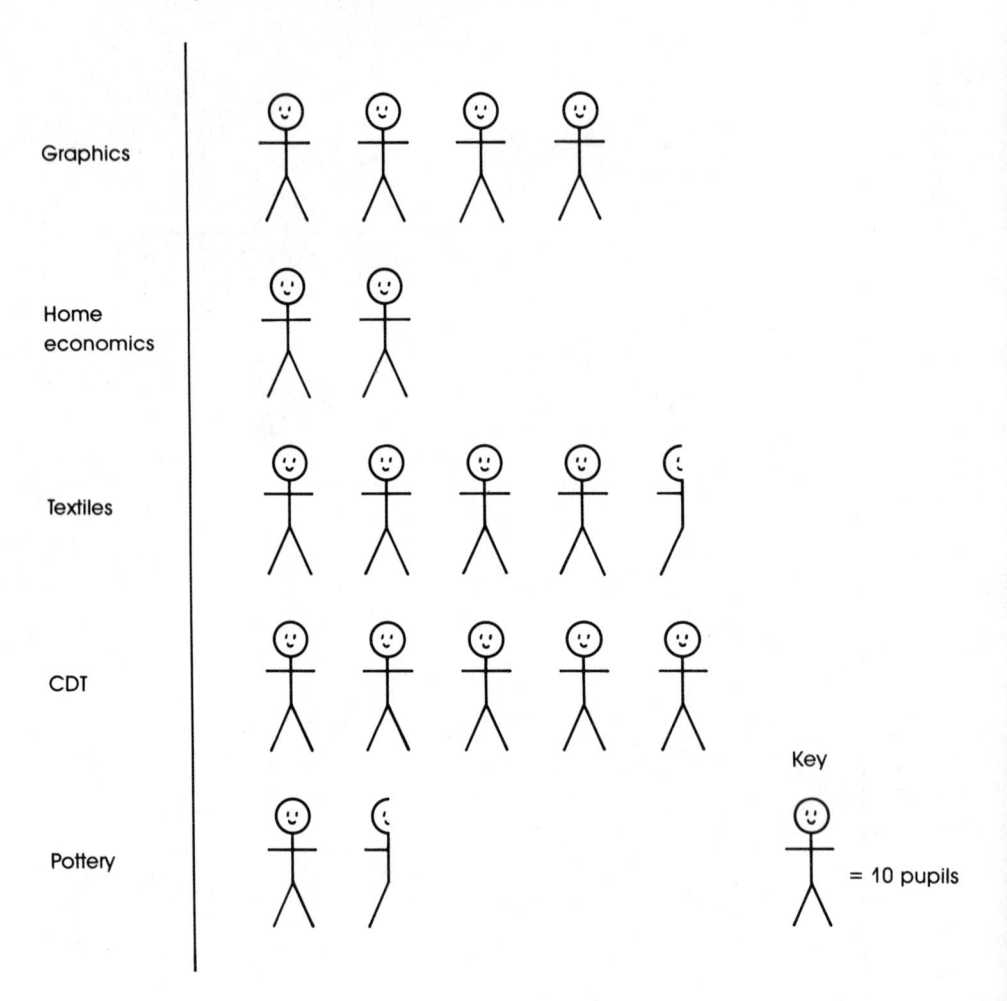

Graphics	4 figures
Home economics	2 figures
Textiles	4 full figures + 1 half figure
CDT	5 figures
Pottery	1 full figure + 1 half figure

Key: 1 figure = 10 pupils

Figure 8.4

(a) How many people chose
  (i) Graphics
  (ii) CDT
  (iii) Textiles?

(b) Which was the least popular subject?

(c) How many pupils were in the group altogether?

Question 5

A survey asked people to state their average incomes. The answers given by men and women are shown separately on this bar graph.

Bar graph to show wages of 240 people by sex.

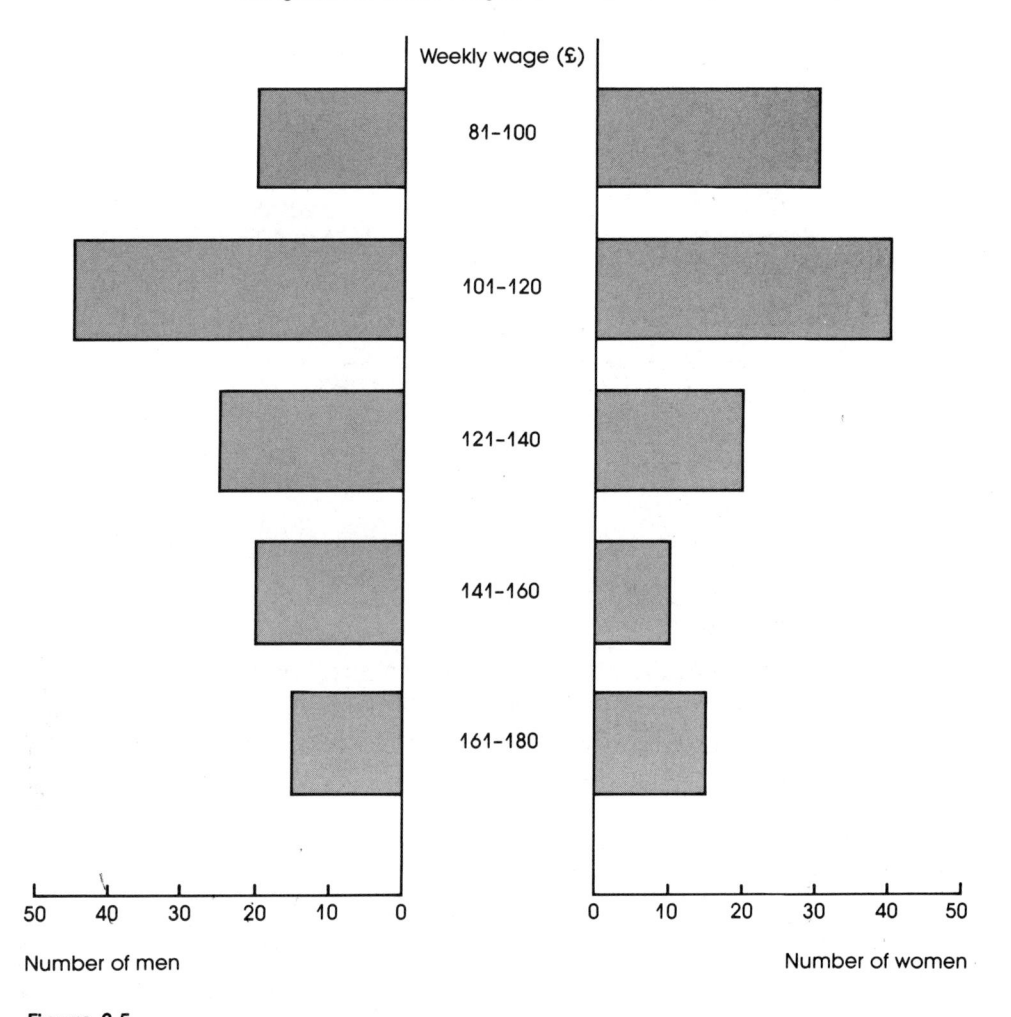

Figure 8.5

(a) Which is the most common wage group for men?
(b) Which is the most common wage group for women?
(c) How many people earned the highest wage?
(d) How many women took part in the survey?
(e) How many men took part in the survey?

CHAPTER 2

Question 6

We surveyed 30 children who owned home computers and asked them which type they had. Here are the results.

C64	CPC464	C64
BBC	Atari 520ST	C128
Spectrum	Spectrum	BBC
C64	BBC	Spectrum
C64	VIC 20	Atari 520ST
Spectrum	Amiga	Electron
Electron	C64	BBC
BBC	Spectrum	Spectrum
Spectrum	C64	Atari 800
Archimedes	Atari 520ST	C64

(a) Copy and complete the following tally chart.

Name	Tally	Freq.
C64		
Spectrum		
BBC		
Atari 520ST		
Others		

(b) Present this data in the form of (i) a bar chart, (ii) a pie chart and (iii) a pictogram.

(c) From which diagram is it easiest to read the number of people with each type of computer?

(d) Which diagram gives the best idea of the smallest and largest sections?

Question 7

In a survey of favourite pop groups and singers taken at the end of 1988, 50 children gave the following answers.

Group/Singer	Freq.
Bros	15
Dire Straits	6
Michael Jackson	11
Phil Collins	5
Wet Wet Wet	8
Others	5
Total	50

This information is to be displayed in the form of a pie chart.

(a) By dividing the 360° of the pie among the 50 people, calculate the number of degrees given to each person.

(b) Calculate the number of degrees for each category. If you round these numbers to the nearest degree, do they total 360°?

(c) Complete the pie chart, labelling it carefully.

Question 8

We went into two comprehensive schools to survey the ages of the teachers. The results were as follows.

St Cronies Comprehensive					St Crankies Comprehensive				
46	23	28	27	29	43	44	38	27	38
34	36	37	53	40	46	43	36	36	49
38	46	27	25	28	31	42	50	53	46
29	26	37	41	28	38	52	28	32	43
42	31	36	30	28	43	27	35	26	29
38	42	26	24	37	32	27	25	27	36
46	25	50	38	32	37	38	35	42	42
30					43				

(a) Produce a stem and leaf plot for each school.

(b) Compare the ages of the two staffs and write down anything you notice about them.

CHAPTER 3

Question 9

We surveyed the prices of some second-hand cars. The results were as follows.

£4800	£4350	£2900	£5300
£4900	£3600	£9600	£8700
£6800	£6700	£6300	£21000
£2100	£7550	£7000	£3650
£2100	£8300		

(a) Using these data, calculate the mean, median and mode.

(b) Which do you think gives the best average for these data? Why?

Question 10

A company marks its bags of crisps 'Average contents 26 g'. Here are some masses of the contents of some packets. Which of the three averages works out as 26 g?

28	27	26	26	27
25	23	27	26	28
30	26	26	28	29
24	25	26	26	28
27	26	25	26	26
27	26	25	24	23

Question 11

The waiting time (in days) for orders to arrive from a mail-order company were recorded as follows.

21	15	16	28	26
22	21	23	20	18
17	27	25	30	18
27	23	16	23	27
28	27	30	26	14
25	24	26	28	28
29	23	19	18	28

(a) Calculate the range of these data.

(b) Calculate the mean, median and mode of the data.

(c) Which of the three averages makes the company seem the fastest?

CHAPTER 4

Question 12

The owner of a small shop is applying to the bank for a business loan. As part of the application, she draws a graph showing her profits over the last six months. Here are the figures.

Jan	£700	Apr	£720
Feb	£680	May	£745
Mar	£725	Jun	£760

Draw a graph for the shop owner which makes her profits look as if they are rising sharply.

Question 13

The following pictogram shows the types of spread used by a sample of people. Look at it very carefully and then answer the questions.

Pictogram to show spreads used by 130 people.

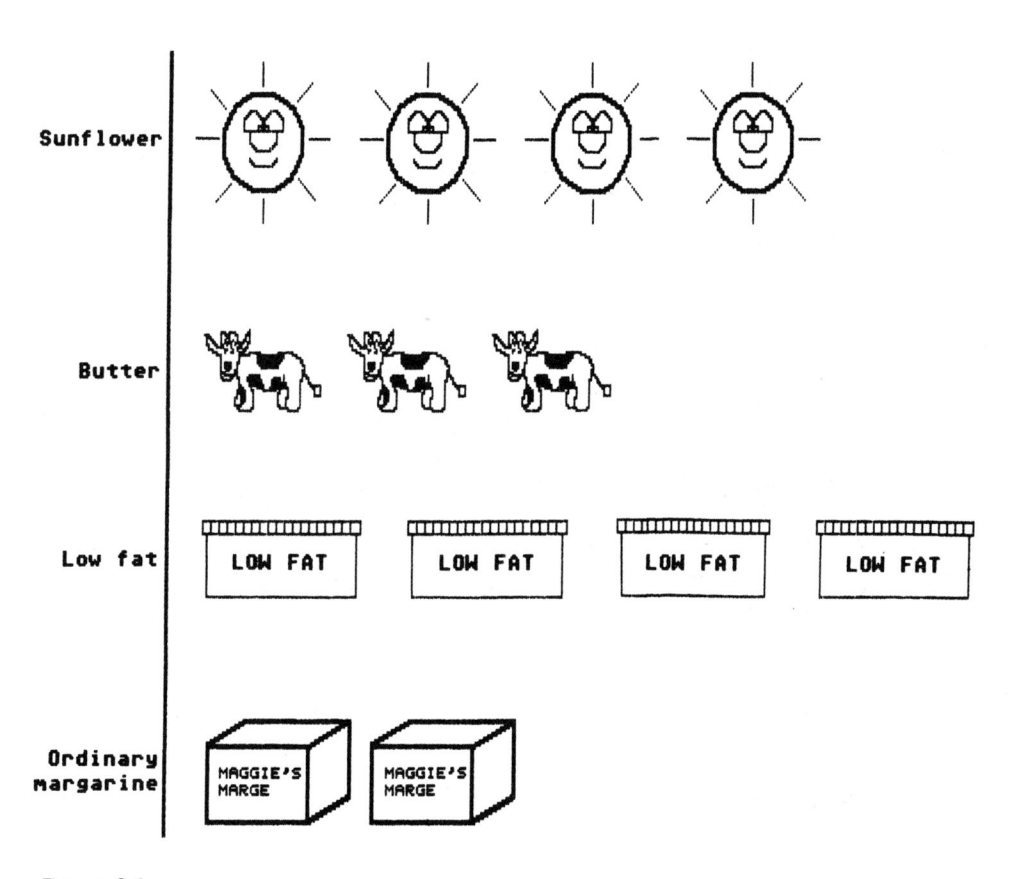

Figure 8.6

(a) Write down all the things which are wrong with the pictogram.
(b) Which of the manufacturers do you think produced this pictogram?
(c) Redraw it so that it obeys all the rules for pictograms.

Question 14

The numbers of calories in three low-calorie drinks are displayed in the following diagram.

Bar chart to show calorie contents of low-calorie drinks.

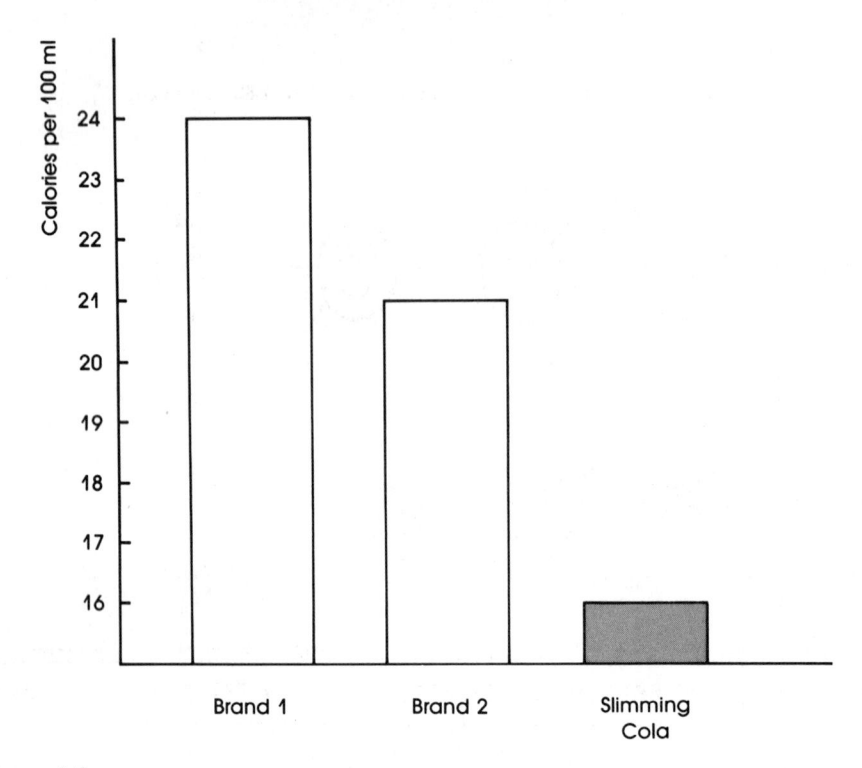

Figure 8.7

(a) Write down all the things which you think are misleading about this diagram.

(b) Redraw the diagram to make it fairer.

Question 15

An investment company wished to show how much its investments had grown during a 15-year period. £5000 invested in 1973 was worth £8300 in 1978, £10 400 in 1983 and £14 600 in 1988. The company chooses to display these figures in a bar chart and naturally wants them to look as good as possible.

Draw the company a bar chart, using any of the techniques you have seen, to make their figures look impressive.

CHAPTER 5

Question 16

The land areas of the four countries of the UK are approximately:

England	130 000 km^2
Scotland	80 000 km^2
Wales	20 000 km^2
Northern Ireland	13 000 km^2

Calculate what percentage each country's area is of the whole of the UK.

Question 17

A computer firm employs 240 men and 150 women. What percentage of each sex does it employ?

Question 18

A survey of 200 children's favourite television sports gave the following results.

Sport	Freq.
Football	48
Rugby	16
Snooker	32
Athletics	46
Cricket	36
Others	22
Total	200

Change the figures to percentages and use them to construct a percentage strip to illustrate the data.

Question 19

Examining a sample of 500 packs of file paper all labelled 'Average contents 500 sheets' revealed that 206 had less than 500 sheets, 53 had exactly 500 sheets and 241 had more than 500 sheets.

Change these figures to percentages and use them to display this information as a percentage pie chart.

Question 20

The following pairs of test results were gained by students in maths and science tests. The maths test was out of 70; the science test was out of 40.

58, 30	30, 24	27, 20	37, 26	43, 27	36, 27
54, 31	43, 31	48, 28	44, 35	56, 29	66, 37
61, 33	65, 34	41, 27	54, 33	56, 32	34, 23
37, 24	51, 30				

(a) Plot the results on a scattergram.

(b) Do you think the results are connected? Explain your answer.

CHAPTER 6

Question 21

The scores of 142 pupils in a maths exam are shown in the following frequency table.

Mark	Freq.	Mark	Freq.
1–10	3	51–60	28
11–20	8	61–70	21
21–30	14	71–80	13
31–40	18	81–90	9
41–50	24	91–100	4

(a) Display this information in the form of a histogram using the intervals shown.

(b) Construct a cumulative frequency table and from it draw a cumulative frequency curve.

(c) Use your graph to estimate the median and to calculate the interquartile range.

(d) The grades for the exam were given as follows.

A	71–100
B	61–70
C	51–60
D	31–50
E	1–30

Construct a second histogram using these class intervals to show the grades.

Question 22

A survey of the houses currently for sale in a small northern English town revealed the following results.

Price (£)	Freq.
Under 20 000	54
20 000–39 999	120
40 000–59 999	158
60 000–79 999	96
80 000–99 999	34

(a) Draw up a cumulative frequency table and use it to draw a cumulative frequency curve.

(b) From your graph, calculate or estimate
   (i) The median
   (ii) The interquartile range
   (iii) The number of houses costing over £90 000
   (iv) The number of houses costing less than £50 000
   (v) The 30th and 70th percentiles.

(c) From the data given above,
   (i) State the modal class
   (ii) Calculate an estimate for the mean house price.

GCSE EXAM-STYLE QUESTIONS

Question 23

Look at the following pie chart which has its angles marked.

Pie chart to show division of £6000 among seven people.

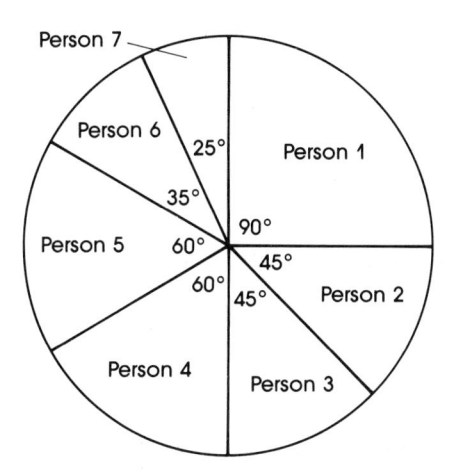

Figure 8.8

(a) What fraction of the money did person 1 get?

(b) Calculate how much money person 2 got.

(c) Who received the least amount of money?

Question 24

The numbers 8, 6, 12, 15, m, have a mean of 10. Find the value of m.

Question 25

The numbers 8, 6, 9, 11, 6, 13, 8, 6, 5, 11, m, have mode 8. What must m be?

Question 26

The heights of 30 children aged 13 were measured (in centimetres). The results were as follows.

159	159	165	157	160	163
159	157	163	168	163	162
163	159	170	165	162	164
165	159	158	154	160	164
159	167	168	169	163	164

Construct a tally chart for these data and then draw a frequency polygon to display them.

Question 27

Pupils' marks in a maths exam were distributed as follows.

Mark	Freq.
1- 10	3
11- 20	10
21- 30	13
31- 40	26
41- 50	32
51- 60	27
61- 70	19
71- 80	15
81- 90	8
91-100	2

(a) Construct a cumulative frequency table and then draw a cumulative frequency curve.

(b) From your graph, obtain an estimate for the median.

(c) Calculate the interquartile range.

(d) Estimate the number of pupils scoring
   (i) 26 or less
   (ii) 75 or less
   (iii) More than 85.

(e) What was the pass mark if 125 people passed?

Question 28

As part of their job applications, 100 workers were asked to take an aptitude test. The times taken were recorded and are shown below.

Time taken (min)	Freq.
1- 2	2
3- 5	15
6- 8	26
9-11	37
12-16	20

Draw a histogram to display the data.

Question 29

A doctor recorded the lengths of his consultations with patients over a period of a week. His findings are recorded below.

Time (min)	Freq.
1-10	23
11-15	19
16-20	9
21-25	6
26-35	3
35-50	1

Construct a histogram to display this data.

Calculate an estimate for the mean time spent with each patient.

Approximately how many patients received more than the mean amount of the doctor's time?

INDEX

Advertising   53, 58
Averages   37, 62

Bar charts   19
Bias   53, 102

Computer databases   107
Continuous/discrete data   22, 89, 91
Cumulative frequency curve   81
   median of   86
   quartiles of   87
   IQR of   88

Data   5, 100
Display of data   8

Frequency   7

Grouped data   42

Histograms   91
   unequal intervals   93

Interpreting diagrams   12

Line of best fit   78

Mean   38, 97
   on a diagram   41
Median   44, 98
   on a diagram   45
Mode   46, 97

Percentages   66
Percentage
   strips   70
   pie charts   72
Pictograms   23
Pie charts   25
   calculations   27
   decimals   29
Problem-solving, stages in   11, 99
Project work   99, 104

Questionnaires   100

Range   48
Reading diagrams   12

Sampling   101
Scales on diagrams   53
Scattergrams   74
Stem and leaf plots   30

Tally   5, 20
TV surveys   2